Preparing to Lead

Narratives of Aspiring School Leaders in a "Post"-COVID World

A Volume in Contemporary Perspectives on Access,
Equity, and Achievement

Series Editor

Chance W. Lewis
University of North Carolina at Charlotte

Contemporary Perspectives on Access, Equity, and Achievement

Chance W. Lewis, Series Editor

Preparing to Lead:
Narratives of Aspiring School Leaders in a "Post"-COVID World (2024)
edited by Patricia Virella, Nathan Tanner, and Darin A. Thompson

Unveiling the Cloak of Invisibility:
Why Black Males are Absent in STEM Disciplines (2023)
edited by Anthony G. Robins, Locksley Knibbs, Ted N. Ingram, Michael N. Weaver Jr, and Adriel A. Hilton

Economic, Political and Legal Solutions to Critical Issues in Urban Education and Implications for Teacher Preparation (2022)
edited by Stephanie Thomas, Shanique J. Lee, and Chance W. Lewis

Imagining the Future:
Historically Black Colleges and Universities—A Matter of Survival (2022)
edited by Gary B. Crosby, Khalid A. White,
Marcus A. Chanay, and Adriel A. Hilton

Equity-Based Career Development and Postsecondary Transitions:
An American Imperative (2022)
edited by Erik M. Hines and Laura Owen

Un-Silencing Youth Trauma: Transformative School-Based Strategies for Students Exposed to Violence & Adversity (2022)
edited by Laurie A. Garo, Bettie Ray Butler, and Chance W. Lewis

Dissertating During a Pandemic:
Narratives of Success From Scholars of Color (2022)
edited by Ramon B. Goings, Sherella Cupid,
Montia D. Gardner, and Antione D. Tomlin

Purposeful Teaching and Learning in Diverse Contexts:
Implications for Access, Equity and Achievement (2022)
edited by Darrell Hucks, Yolanda Sealey-Ruiz, Victoria Showunmi,
Suzanne C. Carothers, and Chance W. Lewis

Reimagining School Discipline for the 21st Century Student:
Engaging Students, Practitioners, and Community Members (2022)
edited by John A. Williams III and Chance W. Lewis

Black Mother Educators:
Advancing Praxis for Access, Equity, and Achievement (2021)
edited by Tambra O. Jackson

Series list continues on next page

The Impact of Classroom Practices:
Teacher Educators' Reflections on Culturally Relevant Teachers (2021)
edited by Antonio L. Ellis, Nathaniel Bryan, Yolanda Sealey-Ruiz,
Ivory Toldson, and Christopher Emdin

Seeing The HiddEn Minority: Increasing the Talent Pool Through Identity,
Socialization, and Mentoring Constructs (2020)
edited by Andrea L. Tyler, Stephen D. Hancock, and
Sonyia C. Richardson

Multiculturalism in Higher Education:
Increasing Access and Improving Equity in the 21st Century (2020)
edited by C. Spencer Platt, Adriel Hilton,
Christopher Newman, and Brandi Hinnant-Crawford

Conquering Academia:
Transparent Experiences of Diverse Female Doctoral Students (2019)
edited by Sonyia C. Richardson and Chance W. Lewis

Community College Teacher Preparation for Diverse Geographies: Implications
for Access and Equity for Preparing a Diverse Teacher Workforce (2019)
edited by Mark M. D'Amico and Chance W. Lewis

Global Perspectives of Issues and Solutions in Urban Education (2019)
edited by Petra A. Robinson, Ayana Allen-Handy,
Amber Bryant, and Chance W. Lewis

Let's Stop Calling It an Achievement Gap:
How Public Education in the United States Maintains
Disparate Educational Experiences for Students of Color (2019)
by Autumn A. Arnett

Responding to the Call for Educational Justice:
Transformative Catholic-Led Initiatives in Urban Education (2019)
edited by L. Mickey Fenzel and Melodie Wyttenbach

Recruiting, Retaining, and Engaging African American Males at
Selective Public Research Universities: Challenges and
Opportunities in Academics and Sports (2018)
edited by Louis A. Castenell, Tarek C. Grantham, and Billy J. Hawkins

Engaging African American Males in Community Colleges: (2018)
edited by Ted N. Ingram and James Coaxum III

Advancing Equity and Diversity in Student Affairs:
A Festschrift in Honor of Melvin C. Terrell (2017)
edited by Jerlando F. L. Jackson,
LaVar J. Charleston, and Cornelius K. Gilbert

Series list continues on next page

*Cultivating Achievement, Respect, and Empowerment (CARE) for
African American Girls in Pre-K–12 Settings: Implications for Access,
Equity and Achievement (2016)*
edited by Patricia J. Larke,
Gwendolyn Webb-Hasan, and Jemimah L. Young

*R.A.C.E. Mentoring Through Social Media:
Black and Hispanic Scholars Share Their Journey in the Academy (2016)*
edited by Donna Y. Ford, Michelle Trotman Scott, Ramon B. Goings,
Tuwana T. Wingfield, and Malik S. Henfield

*White Women's Work:
Examining the Intersectionality of Teaching, Identity, and Race (2016)*
edited by Stephen Hancock and Chezare A. Warren

*Reaching the Mountaintop of the Academy: Personal Narratives, Advice and
Strategies From Black Distinguished and Endowed Professors (2015)*
edited by Gail L. Thompson, Fred A. Bonner, II, and Chance W. Lewis

*School Counseling for Black Male Student
Success in 21st Century Urban Schools (2015)*
edited by Malik S. Henfield and Ahmad R. Washington

Exploring Issues of Diversity within HBCUs (2015)
edited by Ted N. Ingram, Derek Greenfield,
Joelle D. Carter, and Adriel A. Hilton

*Priorities of the Professoriate: Engaging Multiple Forms of
Scholarship Across Rural and Urban Institutions (2015)*
edited by Fred A. Bonner, II, Rosa M. Banda,
Petra A. Robinson, Chance W. Lewis, and Barbara Lofton

*Autoethnography as a Lighthouse:
Illuminating Race, Research, and the Politics of Schooling (2015)*
edited by Stephen Hancock, Ayana Allen, and Chance W. Lewis

*Teacher Education and Black Communities:
Implications for Access, Equity and Achievement (2014)*
edited by Yolanda Sealey-Ruiz, Chance W. Lewis, and Ivory Toldson

Improving Urban Schools: Equity and Access in K–16 STEM Education (2013)
edited by Mary Margaret Capraro,
Robert M. Capraro, and Chance W. Lewis

*Black Males in Postsecondary Education: Examining their
Experiences in Diverse Institutional Contexts (2012)*
edited by Adriel A. Hilton, J. Luke Wood, and Chance W. Lewis

*Yes We Can!
Improving Urban Schools through Innovative Educational Reform (2011)*
edited by Leanne L. Howell, Chance W. Lewis, and Norvella Carter

Preparing to Lead

Narratives of Aspiring School Leaders in a "Post"-COVID World

Editors

Patricia Virella
Montclair State University

Nathan Tanner
University of Illinois at Urbana–Champaign

Darin A. Thompson
Independent Researcher

INFORMATION AGE PUBLISHING, INC.
Charlotte, NC • www.infoagepub.com

Library of Congress Cataloging-in-Publication Data

CIP record for this book is available from the Library of Congress
http://www.loc.gov

ISBNs: 979-8-88730-305-5 (Paperback)

   979-8-88730-306-2 (Hardcover)

   979-8-88730-307-9 (ebook)

Copyright © 2024 Information Age Publishing Inc.

All rights reserved. No part of this publication may be reproduced, stored in a retrieval system, or transmitted, in any form or by any means, electronic, mechanical, photocopying, microfilming, recording or otherwise, without written permission from the publisher.

Printed in the United States of America

Dedicated to the aspiring school leaders
who will lead during these complex times.

CONTENTS

1. Introduction
   Patricia Virella 1

2. Oral Histories as Emancipatory Praxis in School Leadership
   Nathan Tanner 5

3. A Story of Defining Progress
   Ramya Subramanian 9

4. Abnormalities of the Already Abnormal Job of a High School Administrator
   Marissa De Hoyos 19

5. Observational Learning: Examples of School-Based Leadership During COVID-19
   Michael Barbieri 27

6. Teacher Burnout + You: What Can You Do?
   Brenda Chavez 41

7. Collaboration
   Joseph Cashin 53

8. "Because It's Easy"
   Lorin Hannah 61

9. On the Brink of Leaving
   Abigaile Almerido 67

10. From Teacher to Educational Leader: Reflections Upon Educator Identity in the Midst of the COVID-19 Global Pandemic
   Maria Leyson 77

11. Can Anyone Become an Abolitionist Educator?
    April J. Mouton 87

12. Closure
    Darin A. Thompson 109

About the Editors 113

CHAPTER 1

INTRODUCTION

Patricia Virella

In fall of 2021, I began my role as an assistant professor of urban educational leadership at Montclair State University. I was a recent graduate and a former principal who was excited to begin my work training future principals. While I firmly believe that the principalship is the hardest job in the building, I also know that preparing highly effective principals can be one of the most critical pieces of my job. Thus, I began my courses and taught fervently, excited to show my students the great new role they would embark upon. But questions began to pop up during the course, such as "Will we really be able to do this work in our schools?" or "Our schools are struggling to find substitute teachers, so how can I implement a coherent and cohesive curriculum when I don't have consistent teaching staff?" These questions continued, and I began to realize that the principalship, which was already complex and further complicated by the COVID-19 pandemic, was a debilitating crisis. I wondered how as educational leadership professors, we were listening to and responding to these questions. Thus, this book listens to several aspiring leaders to inspire hope, marshal change and acknowledge the complexity aspiring leaders currently face.

Recent scholarship has found that the COVID-19 pandemic has expedited plans to leave the principalship. According to the National Association of Secondary School Principals (2023), 45% of 1,000 school principals surveyed said the COVID-19 pandemic accelerated plans to exit the principalship. To put this into perspective, there are approximately 1,800 public schools in New York City's public school system, including charter schools.

Preparing to Lead:
Narratives of Aspiring School Leaders in a "Post"-COVID World, pp. 1–3
Copyright © 2024 by Information Age Publishing
www.infoagepub.com
All rights of reproduction in any form reserved.

If this estimate were realized in the largest school district in the country, that would leave 810 schools without building administration. This also means that aspiring principals will be entering schools in large numbers, under crisis conditions, expected to lead in ways we know do not prepare them for the principalship.

We approach this book as a way to elevate the voices of aspiring leaders who will enter the field soon, becoming school leaders. Chapter authors discuss both the challenges and opportunities they have experienced due to being in the dual role of aspiring leaders and current educators. Chapter authors also provide poignant feedback on how leadership preparation programs can assist their development as leaders and infuse equity-oriented approaches that mirror their own identity and the educational landscape they will become leaders. One significant contribution of this book is that our authors are from across the continental United States, in both large and small institutions while serving in urban, suburban, and rural school districts. Given the breadth of settings, each chapter will provide poignant suggestions for future aspiring leaders across the nation and educational leadership faculty increasingly trying to meet the needs of the diverse leaders they prepare. Interspersed through the book will be concluding summaries that draw together themes of equity resilience and capture the lessons learned, opportunities presented, and remaining challenges evident in the authors' narratives.

Popular education press and scholarly conversations have focused on the impact of COVID-19 on various aspects of school leadership during the induction process and after. However, voices heard directly from the students are often left out or not heard from in a comprehensive oral historical account. We argue that while the attention is deservingly placed on principals and superintendents in schools leading through the pandemic crisis, there has been less dialogue about the impact of COVID-19 on aspiring leaders who will take the helm amid the lingering crisis. Focusing on this population is explicitly significant as COVID-19, as mentioned above, has disrupted and traumatized many current leaders who will begin to leave the principalship or superintendency en masse. For instance, although in-service leaders are mentoring graduate students' aspiring leaders, their mentors may not still be in their roles as principal or superintendent once the graduates begin their tenure as school leaders in a new school.

The novelty and longevity of COVID-19 has also upended schools across the country. Thus, we are left at the moment when although many students are preparing to be school leaders, those preparing them are not expected to stay. This presents an opportunity for the field of educational leadership to learn from aspiring leaders as to what challenges and opportunities they face to continue developing the field while supporting future graduate students. It is paramount to hear directly from aspiring leaders and learn ways to equip future school leaders better. Thus, *Preparing to Lead: Narratives of Aspiring School Leaders in a Post-COVID World* is positioned to be a must-read for professors looking to support their graduate students in leadership preparation programs as well as for aspiring leader graduate students who are looking for strategies and experiences to navigate their leadership journey during COVID-19.

REFERENCE

National Association of Secondary School Principals. (2023). *NASSP survey signals a looming mass exodus of principals from schools*. NASSP. Retrieved September 20, 2022, from https://www.nassp.org/news/nassp-survey-signals-a-loomingmass-exodus-of-principals-from-schools/#:~:text=Job%20satisfaction%20is%20at%20an,who%20strongly%20agreed%20in%202019

CHAPTER 2

ORAL HISTORIES AS EMANCIPATORY PRAXIS IN SCHOOL LEADERSHIP

Nathan Tanner

> *"The memories of crucial experiences may be re-evaluated and re-contextualized throughout life, but they remain the basis upon which personal memory, and our sense of self-identity, is constructed."*
>
> — Green and Troup (2016, p. 375)

Oral history as both a methodology for capturing human stories and a theory for conceptualizing practices in the world predates contemporary approaches to thinking about the past or contextualizing memories. While still a primary approach to conducting research among and within many Indigenous communities around the globe (Smith, 2021), transmitting knowledge and experience through oral tradition extends into antiquity and transcends geography and notions of class, gender, and race (Vansina, 1985). Furthermore, whether framed as autobiography, oral history, or personal narrative, this approach to capturing the human experience across time and space has also been central to the Black intellectual tradition (Alridge et al., 2021; Franklin, 1995). Historian Aaron David Gresson III, for example, has described an autobiographical approach to narration as "an emancipatory project in dialogic praxis" (Gresson, 2021, pp. 41–42) wherein there is

---

Preparing to Lead:
Narratives of Aspiring School Leaders in a "Post"-COVID World, pp. 5–8
Copyright © 2024 by Information Age Publishing
www.infoagepub.com
All rights of reproduction in any form reserved.

deliberate authorial intention to participate, mediate, and intervene in theoretical debates by using the story of [one's] own intellectual and academic trajectory [or experience] as the source of historiography ... [it has] persisted ... since there is much in social reality that cannot be captured by the traditional analytic tools.... [This method] share[s] an appreciation of the place of subjectivity in the construction of knowledge and the knowable.

Documenting oral histories as a modern research methodology traces its origins in the United States to the Federal Writers' Project in the 1930s and 1940s, which was part of the Works Progress Administration's attempt to gather and preserve accounts of surviving witnesses of enslavement prior to Emancipation at the conclusion of the U.S. Civil War (Sharpless, 2007). Contrary to those contemporary historians who argue oral histories lack "empirical" or "objective" value, oral history as a research methodology has proved crucial to producing historical representations and narrating the experiences of "marginalized or neglected social groups" (Green & Troup, 2016, p. 375) long disavowed by or erased from popular historical records. In the last two decades, oral historians have found poststructuralism, a popular theoretical framework used by educational researchers across the globe, to be a suitable pairing (Peters & Burbules, 2004). In this way, oral history narratives can be approached as "texts," or a form of data, wherein "collective discourses or scripts determine the form of the narrative" (Green & Troup, 2016, p. 381). This allows interviewers—conducting research on their own experiences or those of others—to foreground the "subjectivity in oral testimonies" and take a "subject-centered approach" to research (Green & Troup, 2016, p. 381).

The use of history and oral history to understand school and organizational leadership, although uncommon in 21st century literature on educational and school leadership, it is not unprecedented and has served myriad purposes for educational researchers and practitioners (Gaudi, 2014; Johnson & Pak, 2018; Keulen & Kroeze, 2012). In fact, this approach has a rather long history. Nearly a century ago, acclaimed Black educator Carter G. Woodson, for example, called for educational approaches and pedagogies that sat with and relied on the situated contexts of students' cultures and identities (Woodson, 1933/2005). Since the early-1900s, drawing on self-reflexivity has been a strategy for drawing awareness to the distinctions between "schooling" and "education," understanding human agency, and countering the harmful effects of white dominance, which includes countering "psychic dislocation" (Gresson, 2021, pp. 46–47). In addition, oral histories and personal narratives have allowed educators the freedom to resist the often rigid "structures of the academy," which include the traditional "rules of evidence and academic research and writing" (Span, 2022, p. 14). Finally, oral histories of education and schooling have the added benefit of encouraging contemporary educators to grapple with and even "reform [their] conceptions of the field" of education as they consider the ways our schooling systems have engaged in the historical marginalization of school administrators', teachers', and even students' educational experiences (Rousmaniere, 2004, p. 35).

With this book, it is the editors' intention to further develop oral history as a methodology and as a theoretical praxis for understanding school leadership during moments of crisis. While viral pandemics are not unprecedented in human history, the COVID-19 pandemic is unprecedented in living memory. Therefore, conducting research on and archiving the narratives of school leadership during the global pandemic that began in 2020 and is ongoing as of this writing is imperative. Much can be gained by documenting and interpreting the oral histories of school leadership practice during the past two years that stands to benefit school leaders specifically but educators more generally. This is especially true considering that future school leaders and educators in various positions will likely deal with an increase in global crises.

Readers who engage in this volume will learn from the personal histories of those charged with leading schools throughout the U.S. during a period of immense turmoil and change. Stories about educator burnout, resilience, restoration, as well as evaluating models for approaching educational equity and justice are considered herein. For both the writers in this volume and its readers, these histories have the power to encourage the processing of traumas, the challenging of racism and inequity, and the transformation of individual and systemic approaches to school leadership now and in the future. By foregrounding the past—however recent it may seem—in our present moment, the methods employed here have the power to emancipate educators' leadership praxis and drive us all to new understandings of our identity, especially concerning our place within and across the contours of the United States' complex system of schooling.

REFERENCES

Alridge, D. P., Bynum, C. L., & Stewart, J. B. (Eds.). (2021). *The Black intellectual tradition: African American thought in the twentieth century*. University of Illinois Press.

Franklin, V. P. (1995). *Living our stories, telling our truths: Autobiography and the making of the African-American intellectual tradition*. Scribner's.

Gaudi, R. D., Jr. (2014). *Surviving and thriving in independent school leadership: An oral history study of two enduring and successful school heads in Hawai'i Independent Schools* [Doctoral dissertation, University of Hawai'i at Mānoa]. ScholarSpace Archive. https://scholarspace.manoa.hawaii.edu/bitstream/10125/100515/Gaudi_Robert_r.pdf

Green, A., & Troup, K. (2016). *The houses of history: A critical reader in history and theory* (2nd ed.). Manchester University Press.

Gresson, A. D., III. (2021). Afrocentricity and autobiography: Historiographical interventions into Black intellectual traditions. In D. P. Alridge, C. L. Bynum, & J. B. Stewart (Eds.), *The Black intellectual tradition: African American thought in the twentieth century* (pp. 40–60). University of Illinois Press.

Johnson, L., & Pak, Y. (2018). Leadership for democracy in challenging times: Historical case studies in the United States and Canada. *Educational Administration Quarterly, 54*(3), 396–426.

Keulen, S., & Kroeze, R. (2012). Back to business: A next step in the field of oral history—the usefulness of oral history for leadership and organizational research. *Oral History Review, 39*(1), 15–36.

Peters, M. A., & Burbules, N. C. (2004). *Poststructuralism and educational research*. Rowman & Littlefield.

Rousmaniere, K. (2004). Historical research. In K. deMarrais & S.D. Lapan (Eds.), *Foundations for research: Methods of inquiry in education and the social sciences* (pp. 31–50). Lawrence Erlbaum.

Sharpless, R. (2007). The history of oral history. In T. L. Charlton, L. E. Myers, & R. Sharpless (Eds.), *History of oral history: Foundations and methodology* (pp. 9– 32). Altamira Press.

Smith, L.T. (2021). *Decolonizing methodologies: Research and Indigenous peoples* (3rd ed.). Zed Books.

Span, C. M. (2022). Sam's cottonfield blues. *History of Education Quarterly, 62*(1), 1– 15.

Woodson, C. G. (2005). *The mis-education of the Negro*. Dover. (Original work published 1933)

Vansina, J. (1985). *Oral tradition as history*. University of Wisconsin Press.

CHAPTER 3

A STORY OF DEFINING PROGRESS

Ramya Subramanian

I take a deep breath, and I begin my story. I display the first picture. It is a photo of my parents, who look significantly younger. It looks like it was taken shortly after they got married. My mom is wearing a dark blue sari with gold trim and two long gold necklaces. She has one big red sticker in the middle of her forehead to symbolize marriage and tradition. Her hair is braided into one long braid, and she's wearing jasmine flowers in her hair, while my dad is in a white button-up shirt with black polka dots and thick black glasses. I share how I am the proud daughter of immigrants who came to America from India in the 1980s. I display a picture of a table filled with my mom's delicious Indian cooking and share that I aspire to be an excellent cook like my mom. But I also shared how I always felt nervous about bringing Indian food to school because I could not find the right words to explain what I was eating.

I share that my parents worked tirelessly throughout my childhood to ensure our family had everything my sisters and I needed. But maybe, more importantly, they worked even harder to ensure we did not lose our ties to our culture. I display pictures taken on my many trips to India as a child. In the pictures, I am dressed in Indian clothes, with flowers in my hair, and surrounded by the visible traditions of my proud ancestors. However, I share that despite all of their best efforts, I started to lose the relationship with my cultural identity. I began to assimilate and lose my

---

Preparing to Lead:
Narratives of Aspiring School Leaders in a "Post"-COVID World, pp. 9–18
Copyright © 2024 by Information Age Publishing
www.infoagepub.com
All rights of reproduction in any form reserved.

home language. I lived one identity at home where I was immersed in my parents speaking Tamil, eating Indian food, and wearing Indian clothes. My other identity only spoke English at school, reflecting the identity I saw in the books or lessons I learned. I remember that I felt lonely and did not have anyone to relate with at school. My friends could not understand my cultural traditions, and I did not have the words to help them understand. Without being explicitly told, I always had an underlying expectation from my teachers and peers that I assimilate. And I complied, letting go of my identity my parents worked so hard to ensure I never lost. The final two pictures accompanying my story are of my classroom and students.

Hopefully, my why for becoming an educator is becoming clear to my colleagues. I explain that I first became a teacher because I love working with children. Still, over time, my reason evolved. It became about ensuring that the education we provide our students and community is not subtractive (Valenzuela, 1999) but honors their unique identities and perspectives. More specifically, I envisioned schools in which our students' identities are weaved into their educational experience, rather than being a separate conversation or lesson. I began to form relationships through home visits, and the disconnect between the families' values and what our schools valued became glaringly evident.

I could no longer be complicit in this disconnect.

I take a moment to regain my composure as I say those words. I feel a heavy responsibility to ensure that the students I serve feel honored, valued, and seen in their educational experience. I want to convey this to my colleagues as I tell my story and help them endure this profound but important sense of responsibility.

I take a heavy sigh as I display the last picture from my story, which shows my classroom at my current school. It is bright, colorful, and clean. The students' chairs are upside down on their desks, and a classroom rug is striped with deep shades of red, orange, green, blue, and purple. The rug is against the small classroom library, containing neatly stacked books in small clear plastic bins. The whiteboard is empty except for space with the day's schedule. It is evident that I took this picture before the first day of school, but it also holds so much promise for what is to come that school year. I tell my colleagues that I will continue to advocate for equity in education no matter what it takes because of my deep commitment to our students and families.

I finish my story, and I breathe a sigh of relief. I held onto the feeling for a moment that what I just shared with my colleagues was intimate but also necessary for the work I want us to do together. I notice that my colleagues' faces are full of appreciation and interest. I see them all smiling and expressing gratitude. Then I see one colleague, in particular, take a deep breath in and close her eyes. I glance at the chat box, where the comments begin to roll in. One comment read, "I really appreciate how you brought up how school can sometimes be subtractive, whether we realize it or not. There's subtle pressure to assimilate to a culture that is not like yours because, as kids, we all want to fit in." Another comment reads, "Thank you for talking about the link between your experience and your vision as an educator."

As I respond to the comments and questions from staff, I click on the arrow on my Zoom screen to see the faces of my colleagues, and I notice that one of the teachers is now crying. She ends up turning her camera off for some time while I finish responding to my colleagues. I thank everyone for the opportunity to share my story of self. I explain to them that according to Marshall Ganz, stories of self are narratives that "are an exercise of leadership by motivating others to join you in action on behalf of a shared purpose" (Ganz, 2009). I shared my story with my colleagues to help ground them in my reason for being an educator and advocating for equity. To move us forward as a team, I believe we all had to start grounding ourselves in our experiences and, from there, discover our commonalities and co-construct our purpose for moving forward as a team. At any other time, we would be sharing these stories in person in an authentic way that may or not involve PowerPoint presentations.

Unfortunately, we did not have that choice. We were living through a pandemic, and because of that, all of our interactions happened through Zoom. It was not an ideal setting, but it was the situation we were in, and we had to make it work.

***

I first learned about the experience of sharing my story of self while I was in graduate school for my master's in Emancipatory School Leadership at San Jose State University, which I started in concurrence with my first year as an assistant principal. In my classes, I was diving deep into culturally sustaining pedagogy (Paris, 2012), engaging in conversations centered around community cultural wealth (Yosso, 2005), and deep discussions centered around transforming our education systems. Aside from being exposed to meaningful experiences such as sharing my story of self, the program also fueled me to want to learn everything I could about it what it truly means to be an antiracist and antibiased educator. I was in this program when I became an assistant principal, which allowed me to share my learnings with anyone who wanted to listen. The pandemic had brought to light many of the inequities that existed for so long. I felt that we could no longer ignore these inequities and that we had to confront them with our stories of self as our starting point. My learnings coincided with everything our schools and country were going through during the summer of

2020. Like many organizations at this time, our school network released a statement in support of Black Lives Matter. However, the statement failed to account for the expertise required to facilitate conversations that would sustain this work beyond lip service. It required a confrontation with our biases, history, and how we move forward. If we did not confront our biases and past, we would be opening the door for others to tell our stories. If we don't tell our story, who will?

In early September of 2020, my principal and I co-facilitated a professional development (PD) on implicit bias for our staff. It was a long journey to get us to the point where we could co-facilitate PDs for our team centered around equity, biases, and racial justice. When I approached my principal about facilitating learning spaces for our staff, she presented the idea of us facilitating together and provided me with resources to help with planning. I felt hesitant and wondered if we both could make the intended impact of having our staff acknowledge their biases and how it shows up in their role as educators. I wondered how our staff would receive us, given that as a person of color, I still must co-facilitate with a White individual. Was my principal, as a White woman, in any position to discuss implicit biases and how they impacted our students who primarily identify as BIPOC?

I did not express these hesitations because I was still in the early stages of my time as an assistant principal and was still unsure about leading this session alone. Much of my reflection happened through conversations with the community of individuals who I trusted and would listen to and offer advice. As a result, while in the planning session for the PD, I let her take the lead because I was still navigating how to effectively advocate and make my voice heard in a space where the White voice dominated.

The Friday morning after the PD on implicit biases, my principal asked to chat with me on Zoom to debrief the PD and take the next steps. During this debrief, she shared some feedback from her manager regarding creating space for discomfort when engaging in these PDs. My principal then shared negative self-talk she was engaging in because she believed others were making assumptions about her. She questioned whether as a white woman she was equipped to lead a school in a community that primarily identifies as BIPOC. She acknowledged her privilege to the staff and me on several occasions but worried that our staff would automatically tune her out because of her privilege. This conversation made it evident that we needed to ground ourselves in our stories. Otherwise, we are left making assumptions about others' experiences and beliefs.

Just as our country was grappling with police brutality and the deaths of George Floyd, Breonna Taylor, Ahmaud Arbery, and countless others, my principal was starting to go through her own reckoning. We had several meetings over Zoom where she would process her feelings about White privilege with me. I remembered feeling that, as a person of color, it was not my responsibility to process her feelings. Unlike many in the school community, this is not the first time I grappled with this reality, which placed me in a position to lead the work. However, I became aware of the emotional labor I had to take on as a person of color. There were many times throughout this school year when I found myself crying because I was frustrated. I was frustrated with the labor of being the only person of color on our leadership team, and though I continued to advocate for equity in educational spaces, I was frustrated that I often felt like the only one fighting for actual change. I did not want to be the person to help my principal process her feelings, but I could not figure out how to communicate that to her because, at times, I felt as though I needed her investment in this work to get more folks to listen. Though I often felt the heaviness of this emotional labor, I continued to push through because I kept telling myself that it was for the betterment of the school. I reached out to my community of friends and colleagues who understood my story and knew about my commitment to the work. I relied on them to provide support, advice, and remind me that I needed to take care of myself and my mental health to do this work effectively. I hoped it would eventually lead to the change I desperately wanted to see. Aside from the professional development I planned and co-facilitated with my principal, I continued to advocate for space to process the current events around us. Planned PDs were helpful but did not always leave time to acknowledge and process together. It became exhausting after a while to continue to remind my principal and leadership team that we need time and space for our staff to heal together and that not all of us had the privilege of ignoring the events happening around us. I shared resources with the staff from Learning for Justice, along with any other article, podcast, or film that pushed my thinking. I created a section for these resources in our weekly update to staff every Friday. After a while, though, it became evident that I was not sure if anyone was reading or looking at the resources I shared.

Occasionally, one or two people would respond, but even that left me feeling defeated.

But, despite all of the PDs I was facilitating, the book clubs, and the committees I was engaging in, I continued to live with the feeling that I was not doing enough. I remember learning about the idea of transformative ruptures (Delgado Bernal, 2017) during this time. It is essential to focus on even the smallest of changes because it will eventually lead to the more significant systemic change we want to see. Every day felt like another mountain to climb, and it often felt isolating. When I felt isolated and alone in this monumental task, I had to reach back out and come back to the community of folks who I knew I could rely on to help see the incremental changes I was making.

For me, this community included educators at my school site who I could rely on to advocate for the same things and help me process one-on-one when we needed it. These educators were fellow teachers I befriended before I transitioned to school leadership. Though we were physically apart during the 2020–2021 school year because of the pandemic, and we became even closer during this time. We relied on each other to hold space for one another to process all that was going on, share our frustrations, and allow each other to heal in whatever way we felt was most appropriate at that time. I knew that even though I had moved into school leadership, the divide did not exist between us, and they knew that I was doing everything I could to advocate for tearing apart the inequities that continued to exist. This community gave each other the space to call out white supremacy and how it showed up in our systems and structures as a society and school. It also allowed me to see how much I value community and that this work cannot be done in isolation. With that said, there were times when I did start to feel isolated because my community did not involve fellow school leaders. Because this work often left me feeling isolated, there were many times I wanted to give up and leave my position as an assistant principal. I went through phases where I questioned why enough people did not care about what was happening to the world around us? My frustrations led me to think about it as binary: if folks were not actively involved and a part of the conversation, they were okay with being complicit in the inequities.

Through several conversations with my community of friends and through reflection on the detrimental impacts of cancel culture, I started to consider that everyone is on their journey, and the way they show up to the conversation can vary, but this does not mean that they do not want to listen or understand. This understanding was why our stories of self were essential; they helped us recognize the different reasons and experiences that brought us to this school and this community in particular.

Despite these frustrations and challenges, I continued to grapple with, I continued to push through with planning and co-facilitating additional professional development with my principal. I shared all resources I came across with my staff, hoping to spark interest in a conversation. One staff member, in particular, continued to advocate for unstructured time for us to process all of our feelings together. As a result of this advocacy, the Social Justice Committee was born.

This committee was open to all staff members. However, it was only a select few who attended regularly. My principal joined initially but then stopped attending as we got later into the school year. The majority of the folks who participated in this committee were people of color. During this time, we wrestled with making sense of current events and our place in the history around us. We tried to make sense of the events, how White supremacy played a role in the events, and how to create space to also have these conversations with our students. I continued to process out loud my frustrations with feeling like change was not happening fast enough. Looking back on this time, I am now grateful that we had this time to not only help each other heal through the collective trauma we were experiencing as a community and as people of color. It also allowed me to recognize the little progress we had started to spark.

For example, we recognized that one change we could make was acknowledging the different traditions and holidays that occur at that time of year. We noticed that our staff needed to realize that we should not be centering on holidays like Halloween through conversations and observations. Our staff, students, and families were rich with various traditions we should acknowledge and celebrate. Though it was not much, it was significant for marginalized individuals. I remember using this as an opportunity to speak to the staff about the Hindu holiday of Diwali and that, as a young student, my teachers never acknowledged it. This conversation with the Social Justice Committee felt like another opportunity for me to add to my story to help folks understand why this matters to me and why I am so insistent that we do not continue to be complicit in perpetuating the white supremacist perspective. Here is another piece of my counterstory that challenges the majoritarian narrative. In this space, we all could be vulnerable to each other. We were able to engage in the discomfort and express our frustrations with the state of our country and the education system, and vehemently agreeing that education is political. For the first time in my life, I had a community of people who could openly talk about white supremacy.

This was progress.

I continued to receive emails from colleagues with what they thought were helpful resources, but at the end of the day continued to be band-aids and never directly addressed systemic racism. I thought about the reactions we all received after our stories of self. Was this leading to any greater change or even a shift in individuals' beliefs? Were we giving students the space to acknowledge and show pride in their identity? Or were we continuing with the same marginalized approach I and so many continue to experience in schools across the country? But I saw firsthand that my colleagues who regularly engaged in conversations allowed our students to be themselves and created space for these conversations in their classrooms. This was a small change. This was progress.

I also started to wonder if any of this change was possible without the interest of White folks. I thought about Derrick Bell's idea of interest convergence (Bell, 1980) and if I needed their buy-in before I could get more folks to care. One of the book clubs I engaged in with fellow school leaders was *Planting the Seeds of Equity: Ethnic Studies and Social Justice in the Classroom* by Ruchi Agarwal-Rangnath (2020). This book club, albeit well-intentioned, was started by someone who identifies as white. We engaged in several meaningful discussions that prompted us to consider our roles as school leaders in this journey. However, if I were the one who initiated the book club, would there be as much interest? I am one of many assistant principals in the network and I did not have as much clout. I considered the self-talk I was engaging in myself and questioned if imposter syndrome was keeping me from being more vocal about doing more equity work within our network. I wondered if I was making enough of an impact in moving into an administrative role, and I was not sure if I was impacting the teachers enough for a seismic shift in their instructional approaches. One opportunity was when I wanted to work with the team to infuse the social justice standards into our social studies block.

However, I also repeatedly heard that they desired a curriculum that already incorporated those standards, essentially doing their work. I kept stressing that the work first needed to start with us as adults. We cannot effectively teach students about identity, equity, social justice, and so forth, without having explored these ideas ourselves and confronting our own biases. It was not until our Chief Schools Officer approached me about facilitating a session for our incoming new staff that focused on diversity, equity, and inclusion that I started to realize that folks outside of my school were recognizing me for being a leader in this conversation. I created and facilitated a PD on exploring our identities and provided space for folks to process their identity in triads and how it impacts their role as educators. Though I was nervous about leading the PD for over a hundred people, the feedback I received gave me the confidence to know that this was just the starting point for my journey.

This was progress.

In my story of self, I shared the journey to get to the point where creating equitable educational experiences for all students became my purpose. This journey has involved an incredible amount of reflection on my experiences and what it took to get me here. There were times I experienced a sense of sadness at all of the time lost, and I found myself wanting to return to redefine my identity. My experience in school led to the loss of my identity. For many years, I felt disconnected from who I was at home with my family, with my friends in social circles, and who I was as an educator.

But I also began reclaiming my identity as an Indian American woman. When I shared my story of self, one of my colleagues asked me, "What is one way you are reconnecting with your culture?" I remember hesitating because it was something I was trying to answer myself. I felt guilty for not connecting and losing out on the parts of my identity that my parents worked so hard and sacrificed so much to ensure I never lost. I felt guilty for not being fluent in the language of my ancestors. Tears started to well up in my eyes as I responded to my colleague and said, "I'm brown, and I'm proud."

This response to my colleague elicited a flood of reactions from the rest of my colleagues. I was proudly reclaiming my identity in front of a group of people, something I had never done before. Progress. I started to acknowledge my racial identity by learning more about my family's stories. I became very intentional about the social media accounts I followed; I began cooking more Indian food and even correcting individuals who did not pronounce my name correctly.

Navigating the reclamation of my identity in conjunction with the equity work I was doing as a school leader cemented my motivation for helping others who were also on this journey. I read as many books as possible related to doing equity work in schools. I watched films and webinars and listened to podcasts related to race and the history of marginalized groups, and I started to critically analyze the structures in our education system and society. Returning to my identity allowed me to consider everyone else's stories, which allowed for an even deeper connection with my colleagues. I advocated for teachers to do the same for themselves and their students, but I realized everybody's journey was different. So, my responsibility is to create a space for individuals to collectively work together to process where they are in this journey. I was also progressing. For me, progress looks like remembering that everyone is on a journey of their own. Through listening, reflection, and conversation, I can understand their stories and experiences that led them to where they are now. I no longer view it as you are either with us or against us, but that everyone, to an extent, has some unlearning to do. I call in folks, especially my principal and leadership team, whenever needed and I know that these conversations, no matter how small, are progress.

***

A few weeks later, after my initial story of self, I finished dinner on a cool October evening and decided to check my work emails. I noticed that I received a letter from my colleague who was crying during my story of self. She thanks me for sharing my story, mainly because of its connection to her life. She tells me she found herself looking at the images and thought about her experiences and how they may resonate with her teenage daughter. "Your story also resonated with me because your story gave me insight into the struggles that my daughter might face or currently faces," she says. I take a deep breath, and my eyes fill with tears as I finish reading her email. This email and the reactions I received from my colleagues provides proof that this is why equity work is essential in schools. And why we need to devote more time to holding space for conversations about our stories and experiences. It is easy for educators to get caught up in just thinking solely about our students' academic needs. This colleague's reaction brings the need to dig deeper into our real purpose for becoming educators and what we believe about our children and their identities. Above all, it validates the need for this work to be a collective effort. We cannot and should not do this alone.

I decided to stay on as an assistant principal because I realized that I could have that greater impact I initially hoped for when I started this position. There are times when it becomes challenging to push through, especially when you do not see the progress right away. Ultimately, I come back to the picture of my parents that I shared in my story of self. I think about their sacrifice and all that they did, and continue to do, to help my sisters and me, along with my niece and nephew, hold on to our traditions and our values. They traveled halfway across the world with the hopes of creating a better life for themselves and their children. I think about the students, families, and the community I serve. I consider their culture, their values, and all that makes their traditions rich and beautiful. The road to transforming education is a long one and is not without bumps. However, this road is not one that I can continue down alone. It is one that I must march down with the collective effort of the individuals who are also committed to transforming education. Together, we will lift up those transformative ruptures (Delgado Bernal, 2017) for everyone to see. Together, we will honor our unique identities and understand that everyone has their story that brought them to where they are now. As future ancestors, we will disrupt these systems and pave a new way forward. We will continue to tell our stories so that, collectively, we will progress on this journey together.

REFERENCES

Agarwal-Rangnath, R., & Camangian, P. (2020). *Planting the seeds of equity: Ethnic studies and social justice in the K–2 classroom*. Teachers College Press.

Bell, D. A. (1980). Brown v. Board of Education and the interest-convergence dilemma. *Harvard Law Review, 93*(3), 518. https://doi.org/10.2307/1340546

Delgado Bernal, D. (2017). A testimonio of critical race Feminista Parenting: Snapshots from my childhood and my parenting. *International Journal of Qualitative Studies in Education, 31*(1), 25–35. https://doi.org/10.1080/09518398.2017.1379623

Ganz, M. (2009). *What is public narrative: Self, us, and now*. Retrieved 2020, from https://dash.harvard.edu/bitstream/handle/1/30760283/Public-Narrative-Worksheet-Fall-2013-.pdf

Paris, D. (2012). Culturally sustaining pedagogy. *Educational Researcher, 41*(3), 93–97.

Valenzuela, A. (1999). Introduction. In *Subtractive schooling: U.S.-Mexican youth and the politics of caring* (pp. 3–32). State University of New York Press.

Yosso, T. J. (2005). Whose culture has capital? A critical race theory discussion of community cultural wealth. *Critical Race Theory in Education*, 69–91. https://doi.org/10.1080/1361332052000341006

CHAPTER 4

ABNORMALITIES OF THE ALREADY ABNORMAL JOB OF A HIGH SCHOOL ADMINISTRATOR

Marissa De Hoyos

This year has been far from normal. At the time Governor Abbot mandated that all schools open for the 2021–2022 school year, the hope of many was that "things would go back to normal." Ironically, the reality is that that particular statement could not be the furthest thing from the truth. The beginning of this school year also meant the beginning of my 24th year in education and my 11th as an assistant principal. Up to this point, there was very little I could say that I had not seen or heard before. This year has definitely been different. Upon returning, the administrative team has mainly dealt with discipline issues relating to COVID-19 and the social-emotional impact of students coupled with the normal teenage issues of dating and overbearing parents.

This year we have dealt with behaviors requiring more than a simple consequence of in-school or out-of-school suspension or alternative school placement. This year, each situation requires an in-depth discussion with the student to better understand their background. Each student needed the opportunity to share their story that provided insight into their behaviors, regardless of the specific behavior. Students were returning from a year and a half of virtual learning with issues they still need help addressing. It is my opinion that they are simply not equipped with the proper tools to deal with what life has thrown their way in the last few years.

In fact, this rings true for both teachers and administration alike. Not all adults are handling the pandemic well. Teachers are feeling overwhelmed with new requirements and adjusting back to being face-to-face. Texas House Bill 4545 requires that every student receives 30 targeted instruction hours for each failed state standardized test in addition to the normal instruction. Teachers also struggled with facilitating student-centered instruction versus placing the desks in rows and simply having the students complete an assignment online for the students to complete on their own as they had previously done during the pandemic. Administrators are struggling also with enforcing the Student Code of Conduct for students who have not needed to dress appropriately, not sit in a desk for 45 consecutive minutes minimum, not and supporting an academic campus while still showing compassion for the student, the teacher, and themselves.

DEFINITION OF COMPASSION

"Compassion is about finding the balance between sympathy—feeling for someone, and empathy—feeling with someone. It is as neuroscientist Max Planck says, 'experiencing feelings of loving kindness toward another person's affliction'" (Jack, 2017, p. 13). The world is dealing with the pain and trauma of the pandemic, and we as leaders need to find some compassion if we want to survive as an assistant principal, a teammate, and within ourselves.

COMPASSION FOR STUDENT

As an assistant principal, there are different elements that need to be taken into consideration when deciding on how to appropriately discipline a student that is suspected of breaking the Student Code of Conduct. I approach the situation as a campus leader and a teacher. The expectation as an administrator is to ensure that all students are in compliance with the student code of conduct approved by the district school board, though the style of leadership is my individual responsibility. As a leader, I also approach a situation as a teaching opportunity with the lesson to be determined based on the student and the situation. When deciding on the most appropriate lesson, I must remember that the student is an adolescent living in the middle of a pandemic, which is a historical event that no living adult has had to deal with prior to this event. In a study conducted on the impact of COVID-19 on adolescents, the researchers found that "as the pandemic continues, there is an urgent need to monitor students' mental health and to examine how school teaching modalities and infection mitigation strategies influence the mental health of adolescents" (Gazmararian et al., 2021, p. 367). These various perspectives require the synthesis of leadership, educational, and psychological disciplines to approach the situation as an educational leader who is cognizant of the characteristics of an adolescent.

My current pride and joy is Genesis (a pseudonym). She was first brought to my attention when a parent reached out with concern that a young girl was taking selfies in the school bathroom of herself smoking a vape pen. It did not take long to identify the student. My male discipline partner and I, John, brought her in to question her behavior. Our heart immediately broke and we went into parent-mode. We knew we could not truly adopt her, but we agreed to pseudo-adopt her. She shared with us that her biological mother gave her up for adoption when she was merely a toddler. Another woman graciously adopted her and had been raising her until COVID arrived. The adopted mother felt the pressure of having an excessive amount of people in a house during a pandemic when no one was allowed to really leave their houses. Her solution was to drop Genesis off a behavioral center and never return. When Genesis turned 18, she was able to release herself. It was at that time that she decided to enroll herself back in school as an unaccompanied youth to finish her high school years and earn her diploma. John and I have spent many hours throughout this year talking and coaching her on making the right decisions and planning for the future. We are happy to announce that we just ordered our psuedo-child's cap-n-gown, and she plans on graduating in June. We by no means cured her of all her ailments, but we did show her some compassion that I believed made school a safe place to learn. She simply needed to believe that people could be trusted. Jack (2017) wrote:

> The difference between acknowledging and fixing is that fixing shuts people down, while acknowledging keeps the communication open. Compassion is all about trying to understand other people's stories, and acknowledgement is the first step. We can't even begin to understand their story if we are in the midst of trying to fix them. (p. 16)

COMPASSION FOR TEAM

Every year as an administrator, I have had to work with a different team. Every year there are changes due to one or more of the administrators that have moved from one campus or another, have left the district, or left the world of academia completely. This year alone, I have seen all three situations come to fruition. The job satisfaction of assistant principals (AP) is linked to the success of districts, campuses, and ultimately the students themselves. Bartanen et al. (2021) researched the mobility rate of APs and found the rate to be higher than that of teachers or principals. They also found that "APs in high-poverty schools are substantially more likely to change schools and exit school leadership" (p. 376). Bartnen et al. also affirms the link between principal turnover increasing the likelihood that APs would exit school leadership or change schools to hurt school performance. School administrators have historically expected to place the needs of others first. Combined with high demands and limited resources, they have experienced stress and burnout. DeMatthews et al. (2021) stated, "Not surprisingly, repeated principal turnover on a campus is likely to have a deleterious effect on student achievement and school working conditions" (p. 159). With as much change as is associated with the job of assistant principal, it is essential to contribute to building a team. A strong team is a major component of a successful school year. With an abnormal school year such as this, it is the team that will help with investigations and support. The team spends more time together than they spend with their own families, which makes it essential for the team to work coherently.

    This school year, I returned to the campus where I first started my career in teaching straight out of college. As an assistant principal, we become accustomed to frequently being moved from one campus to another. This means learning the dynamics of the team you are joining and building a relationship with them. This year was no exception. I joined an AP team with three males, two with many years of experience, John and Andrew, and one who had just started this position this school year, William. From the day the school doors opened in August, I felt like we were literally running the whole day. We were breaking up fights, investigating smoking in the restroom, students walking the halls for hours refusing to go to class, and students leaving our closed campus to go get a taco. We had no time for deep discussions or checking on each other's social well-being. We barely had ten minutes to inhale a lunch that may have been heated up a few times, because another situation had to be dealt with before we were able to actually eat. We were running until at one of our regular scheduled Tuesday administrative meetings in December, our principal starts with "William has something to share with us." William announced that he was leaving the profession completely. He had come to the realization that the world of academia was not for him, and Friday would be his last day. We were stunned and sat in awkward silence for what seemed awhile until Andrew responded for the team when he said, "We wish you the best." For weeks we talked about what had happened. We questioned what we could have done differently or whether there were any signs of distress that we missed. I believe Brené Brown's in *Dare to Lead* (2018) may have our answer when she states, "Courage is contagious. To scale daring leadership and build courage in teams and organizations, we have to cultivate a culture in which brave work, tough conversations, and whole hearts are the expectation, and armor is not necessary or rewarded" (p. 12). We needed to stop and talk about a situation that despite all our years of experience had not dealt with ourselves. We needed to show our vulnerability.

COMPASSION FOR SELF

In addition to having compassion for others, we should have compassion for ourselves. Jack (2017) states:

> While what we go through is unique and important, self-compassion helps us acknowledge that what we have been through is nothing to be ashamed of or kept to ourselves. It allows us to embrace our pain and realize that we are not alone.... The reality is that our suffering is what connects us all. (p. 59)

Similarly, Brown (2018) identifies a pivotal moment in her own leadership growth was when she "was comfortable enough to use the right language and say, 'Are you lonely?' I may be able to create a connection where maybe, just maybe, they will come and talk to me" (p. 62). So many times in my life, I have asked the good Lord why I had to experience what I had to experience throughout my life. Life has not been fair or good to me. My mother always gave me words of encouragement and would acknowledge that I did seem to struggle more than others but that I needed to hang on. She believed when good things happened, I was going to be that much more appreciative for what I had. Now that I am older, I find myself sharing my stories with others who find themselves struggling with life's cruelties. I find that sharing my stories allows for a connection to be made making the other person feel comfortable enough to share their story, which gives me a glimpse into how I can help them. A prime example is a student named Diana who loves to fight. She does not need much of a reason. If anyone looks at her or any of her friends or family the wrong way or for too long of a period, the fight is on. She is very dramatic and speaks with her hands, almost as much as her mouth. Recently, she was in my office ranting about how mad she was and how she wanted nothing more than to hit another little girl's face. I shared with her my crooked fingers and how when I was young, I had the same energy and uncontrollable anger. I told her how embarrassed I was to even share that story, but that there came a time when I realized that my anger was actually hurting myself more. I hated the person I used to be and never wished to go back to that person. Life is more peaceful with who I am today. Diana sat and listened to my story, and said "Miss, I need help controlling my anger." Those were the magic words. I could then introduce Diana to communities in school, whom I am confident can help this young lady before she finds herself in legal trouble for assault changes in the future. If they cannot help Diana themselves, they certainly know people who can. Merely sharing this story reminds me that my struggles have served a purpose. I needed to show myself some compassion and grace for who I was and be grateful that my past can help students now.

CURE SELF

Having compassion for students, your team, and yourself requires that a person faces their demons. If a person has any unresolved issues that have been suppressed, regardless of their mantra of being out of your mind and out of your sight, they will resurface. Issues will resurface the instant another human being hits a nerve and forces the person to recall all past hurts. "The difference—the delta—between what we make up about our experiences and the truth we discover through the process of rumbling is where the meaning and wisdom of this experience live" (Brown, 2018, p. 267). Unresolved issues make it extremely difficult to have compassion for anyone, including oneself. There are several ways to deal with one's issues. This may be through a local church that offers classes, such as Peeling Back the Onion. You could also seek one-on-one help from a therapist or psychiatrist. In more severe and specific cases, the 12-step program can be tremendously helpful. The program is not merely for alcohol or drug addiction. It is also for other issues that a person may be struggling to deal with in their life. Becoming the best version of you contributes to becoming a strong leader that can have the compassion needed as an assistant principal. Educational Service Center in Region XX now even offers a three-day workshop based on a book by Brené Brown (2018) entitled *Dare to Lead*, a guide to being a courageous leader. She describes leadership as "anyone who takes responsibility for finding the potential in people and processes and who has the courage to develop that potential" (p. 4). Thus, in order to be a courageous leader in the position of assistant principal during a pandemic, we are going to have to first ask ourselves some difficult questions, in order to be able to ask how we can help others.

REFERENCES

Bartnen, B., Rogers, L. K., & Woo, D. S. (2021). Assistant principal mobility and its relationship with principal turnover. *Educational Researcher, 50*(6), 368–380.

Brown, B. (2018). *Dare to lead: Brave work, tough conversations, whole hearts.* Random Press.

DeMatthews, D., Carrola, P., Reyes, P., & Knight, D. (2021). School leadership burnout and job-related stress: Recommendations for district administrators and principals. *The Clearing House: A Journal of Educational Strategies, Issues and Ideas, 94*(4), 159–167.

Gazmararian, J., Weingart, R., Campbell, K., Cronin, T., & Ashta, J. (2021). Impact of COVID-19 pandemic on the mental health of students from 2 semi-rural high schools in Georgia. *Journal of School Health, 91*(5), 356–369.

Jack, L. (2017). *The compassion code: How to say the right thing when the wrong thing happens.* Kat Biggie Press.

CHAPTER 5

OBSERVATIONAL LEARNING

Examples of School-Based Leadership During COVID-19

Michael Barbieri

BeepBeep**Beep**

I grabbed my phone from the nightstand table, turned off my alarm, and looked across the room to see the clock beaming "8 A.M." I would have been running late during any normal school day prior to this point in the year. My heart would have instantly jolted and then surely dropped into my stomach. However, this spring was proving itself to be far from normal. Instead of frantically throwing off the covers and rushing through my morning routine, I pulled myself out of bed at a leisurely pace, tossed on a school spirit shirt, and meandered to the living room sofa. Another day of teaching elementary music remotely required a fully charged laptop, one pair of headphones, and an extra-large cup of coffee. The floor was littered with instrument cases, piles of sheet music, and beginner band methods books. The few trips around my one-bedroom apartment meant that my morning commute was finished, and the school day did not even start for another hour.

Throughout the remainder of the day, I had minimal interactions, if any at all, with my colleagues or administrators. Other than seeing and speaking with my students through the miniature windows of a zoom call, I held music lessons in what felt like a vacuum. Separated from the rest of the school, and void of the type of human connection that typically occurs in education on a daily basis. "We can't hear you, I think you're muted" or "Did you get disconnected from the meeting?" became the phrases that quickly formed my new virtual teaching vernacular. Due to the spread of COVID19, eventually leading to the closing of schools throughout the country, the hallways, classrooms, and desks of our building felt distant, as if off in space on another planet. The educational world was completely knocked off-kilter, and everyone in the field had no choice but to buckle up for the ride as we acclimatized to the era of the "new normal."

This scene replayed almost every day on loop during the spring of 2020, the beginning of the COVID-19 pandemic. "Earlier this year, COVID-19 slammed the door firmly shut on all aspects of everyday life" (Harris & Jones, 2020). Throughout the early stages of the pandemic, I was, and still remain a public-school music educator, teaching music to students in Grades 3 through 5 at two elementary schools. It goes without saying that the emergence and spread of the coronavirus completely altered the landscape of education in an incalculable way for teachers, students, and communities throughout the world. "It has redefined learning as a remote, screen-based activity limiting most learners to online teacher support" (Harris & Jones, 2020). While grappling with the impact of the virus on the teaching side of education, I was also completing my master's degree in educational leadership. Throughout my degree program, I was focused on gaining real-life knowledge and experience to better understand school-based administration, with the ultimate goal of becoming a transformative educational leader in the future. "Prior research reveals that school leaders' sensemaking is influenced by their content knowledge, professional preparation, and experiences, identity and personal experiences, district and school context, and policy mandates" (Maloney & Garver, 2020, pp. 85–86). While the roles and responsibilities of school principals are constantly evolving, the adaptive leadership practices exercised by school administrators during the pandemic allowed me to progress my leadership identity beyond conventional norms and strengthen my capacity to effectively respond when the world shifts in an unforeseen way.

As a preservice educational leader, the pandemic critically influenced, both positively and negatively, my opportunities to observe, analyze, and reflect on the behaviors of administrators in my school district. In many ways, COVID-19 and the nature of teaching virtually from home severely limited my ability to learn from my principals' leadership. "Unfortunately, the global dispersion of this pandemic and those treating it, alongside the mandate to practice greater social distancing to curb the disease's spread, make it difficult to enact policies to encourage interpersonal learning interactions" (Myers, 2020, p. 3). While Myers is referring to the virus's impact on professional learning in the healthcare industry, the same analysis can be applied to its effect on the learning process within the field of education. It has been equally difficult as a teacher to gain the real-world knowledge needed to become an effective leader due to the social and physical distancing protocols that coincided with the virus's development. "The staff meetings, coffee catch-ups, and corridor chats with colleagues that made up a school day have gone" (Harris & Jones, 2020). Furthermore, during this time, the duties and responsibilities of a school principal were transitioning to meet stakeholders' unique needs during the pandemic, making it difficult for a preservice leader to rely on the established norms one would have been familiar with pre-COVID-19.

In contrast, I was also provided with the unique lens to watch my school leaders adapt to the stressors of the pandemic in both a creative and inventive fashion. "By adopting an adaptive approach to leadership, school leaders can build resiliency and capacity for their school communities to weather future disruptions caused by the pandemic" (Bagwell, 2020, pp. 30–31). Principals and building administrators were forced to discover diverse approaches to school leadership and renovate the educational systems they had once relied on in the years of stability before the outbreak of the COVID-19 virus. "In such disruptive times, school leaders cannot emulate the leadership practices they witnessed or enjoyed in a period of stability, continuity, and relative calm" (Harris & Jones, 2020). Observing these occurrences during an unprecedented pandemic provided the opportunity, as an aspiring leader, to reflect and hypothesize on a school-based leader's overall role and responsibilities. Additionally, devoting time to ruminate about these experiences allowed me to consider how I would have begun to handle a crisis's remarkable challenges if I were a school leader. The examples in this chapter offer a perspective for future and current leaders to consider in the aftermath of the COVID-19 pandemic.

Observational Learning

Albert Bandura (1986) is noted with the evolution of the social cognitive theory as a development of the social learning theory (Grusec, 1992). Social cognitive theory affirms that much of the learning process takes place deliberately or unconsciously by observing behaviors and the emerging outcomes from these observations (Bandura, 1999). This learning process has come to be known as observational learning. "It explains learning as a continuous interaction between cognitive, behavioural, and environmental influences" (Groenendijk et al., 2013, p. 4). For example, many infants learn to eat with utensils by watching an adult. First, the action of eating with the tools is observed and then eventually imitated by the child. While many often associate observational learning with children, its more frequent use can be utilized at all developmental stages throughout life. Recently, a close friend broke down on the side of a highway with a flat tire. Having never changed a tire in their life, and the mechanic service estimated a two-hour wait time, they searched for a tire changing video on their phone, reviewed the steps, and then proceeded to change the tire with the spare in the trunk. Through observation of the video, they were able to emulate the skills needed to complete the task. I am confident that with the instant access to the knowledge offered by smartphones and other technologies, utilizing the benefits of observational learning has become commonplace for many. Just the other day, I was able to learn how to make a new pasta sauce without following any written recipe, as one traditionally would. By watching steps in a condensed 30-second clip on my phone, I was able to prepare the meal just by visually following along. Think of a time when you may have recently utilized observational learning to acquire a new skill, solve a problem, or reach a goal.

Before participating in an internship, all aspiring leaders can benefit from observing and analyzing administrators' behaviors at all levels as a powerful tool to enhance practical knowledge and develop a deeper understanding of educational leadership. "In essence, social learning through observation provides invaluable shortcuts to leadership development" (Kempster, 2009). Another portion of Bandura's social cognitive theory deals with the concept of self-efficacy. It refers to an individual's belief in his or her capacity to execute behaviors necessary to produce specific performance accomplishments (Bandura, 1977). It can also impact the observer's perceived level of difficulty in regard to completing tasks. "People with high assurance in their capabilities approach difficult tasks as challenges to be mastered rather than as threats to be avoided" (Bandura, 1994). It can be argued that having the opportunity to view an effective model of skill, task, or behavior successfully can help raise the self-efficacy of aspiring school leaders. In turn, this can play a large role in the observer's motivation and perception of difficulty surrounding the responsibilities and duties of a school administrator.

The Challenge

During the first wave of the pandemic, one's ability to observe quality school-based leadership was severely hindered due to lack of access. For example, principals and building administrators were not able to be observed in their everyday roles due to the very nature and limitations of virtual learning. Being physically removed from the learning environment made it impossible to get a firsthand view of a principal's dialogue with an upset parent/guardian, to note behaviors as they provided observational feedback to a newly hired teacher, or to internalize the steps taken to effectively run a fire drill.

> All those informal, important, moments where social relationships are built, and leadership is enacted simply vanished overnight. Parents, students, and teachers now exist in a twilight education world either awaiting the return of normal service or hoping for some new normal that might offer stability, continuity, and reassurance. (Harris & Jones, 2020)

To be clear this is not to say that school leaders did not make every effort to remain involved in the learning process or stay visible to teachers and students. But they were required to shift focus toward a crisis management style of leadership. "Instead, all school leaders will need to be engaged in constant crisis and change management which will require support and collaboration from all staff" (Harris & Jones, 2020). As I suspect that the future will bring a higher level of crisis-related situations in schools, management of emergency situations will become a more common responsibility for school leaders to confront. It is my ultimate goal to provide aspiring leaders with the opportunity to reflect on their own future approaches to leadership as we continue to deal with the ramifications of the pandemic.

School Culture

> *"Good Morning! I hope you are all doing well and are ready for another fabulous day of school. The weather is a high of 55 degrees and partly cloudy with a chance of rain in the afternoon. Today is our 35th day of virtual learning and I am so proud of our school and what we have accomplished since we have started learning from home. Let's stand up and say the pledge of allegiance…"*

I stood up at my living room table and recited the pledge while a photo of the American flag was displayed on the screen. My principal then continued to give the morning announcements and further commended our students on their success with transitioning to virtual learning. He concluded the video with a positive demeanor and optimistic tone by announcing, *"Even though we cannot be together right now, your teachers and I are still here to help you however we can. I am so impressed by all of your accomplishments these last few weeks and I know that this will be our best day of learning yet."* Like clockwork, a new morning announcement video appeared in every virtual classroom to greet students, teachers, and families to another day of remote school.

As the pandemic raged, the videos became more developed and engaging, as did the show's star. A slideshow with curated graphics accompanied my principal on screen, music from a variety of genres always played in the background, and eventually, a joke of the day was told. Cinco de Mayo was celebrated, daily trivia questions tested students' knowledge, and props, like hats, sunglasses, and instruments, were added into the mix. Students and teachers alike waited each morning in anticipation for the video, like looking forward to the release of your favorite television show. After reflecting on the videos almost two years later, I realized the most significant component was not necessarily the content of the videos or the flashy graphics, but the school leader who continued to hold out hope for students, created stability however possible and placed an emphasis on student well-being through learning.

It is well-established that the school principal, as the main educational mouthpiece, has a colossal influence on a building's climate and culture. "The attitude and priorities of the person in charge bounce off the other people in the setting and could be repeated many times, perhaps at no one's conscious awareness level" (Pawlas, 2013, p. 30). Allowing a negative school culture or climate to reside within a building is the most serious threat to the success of an institution of learning. "There were significant differences in school climate between successful and unsuccessful schools, even when taking into account schools' student characteristics and resources" (Voight et al., 2013, p. 27). The pandemic, accompanied by its isolating attributes, pressed educational leaders to find new approaches to strengthening the school climate for the overall well-being of staff and students. Weiner et al. (2021) noted:

> While there are many striking aspects to the COVID-19 pandemic, the scale and rapidity with which educators had to respond to school closures and fundamentally shift all aspects of their work is unparalleled. School principals, tasked with leading this transition, were thrust into the role of helping faculty, staff, students, and families learn how to effectively "do school" in a highly uncertain and ever-changing environment. (pp. 1–2)

With no formal playbook for dealing with the unprecedented situation, these daily videos were just one way my principal worked to remain visible to the school community and maintain a positive culture. Brion (2021) noted, "leadership in times of crisis is about dealing with events and emotions in ways that minimize personal and organizational harm" (p. 164). By modeling a business-as-usual attitude and celebrating wins while simultaneously acknowledging the struggles of daily learning in the new virtual model, this school leader was able to guide and support the community from behind their desk each morning. Ironically, literature regarding educational leadership generally discourages school leaders from remaining in their offices throughout the day. But during the age of COVID-19, we learned that principals had the ability to be present and available to the school community without ever getting up from their office chairs.

As we continue to understand the negative effects of the pandemic, aspiring school leaders will need to continue to innovate and improve upon the traditional methods of building a healthy school climate. In my opinion, a silver lining is that the pandemic has given and will continue to give, current and future leaders the unique pathway to reset/reframe school climates to better address the inequities damaging to marginalized populations of learners prior to the school shutdowns. "For example, these policies and plans should address how educators will serve marginalized groups of students such as English learners and students with mild to severe disabilities in all environments: brick and mortar, remote learning, and blended learning (Brion, 2021, p. 179). With such a large disruption to learning, leaders must work to secure the inclusion of each learner, especially vulnerable student groups disproportionately affected by school closures. A robust school climate will provide all students with equal access to appropriate grade-level content, instruction, resources, and environments. By reflecting on past practices, educational leaders can seize this opportunity for school climate improvement to benefit overall student wellness and achievement. As the country has experienced drastic transformations, so should the visions within our schools to meet the needs of every student and family.

Communication

Clear and consistent communication has, and always will be, a foundational pillar of effective school leadership. Without an established system of communication, it would be extremely difficult for even the most capable leaders to steer all stakeholders through a crisis. Kaul et al. (2020) explains, "Even after these basic needs were addressed, principals faced overwhelming logistical hurdles of ensuring technology access and establishing clear communication streams" (p. 1). The necessity to practice physical and social distancing during the pandemic demanded principals and administrators utilize a plethora of communication methods to connect with staff, students, and families. "Firstly, in the period leading up to the school closures and move to online learning, leaders reported that it was essential to be both regular and clear in their communications" (Longmuir, 2021, p. 8). Consistent and honest communication from school leaders offered stability when procedures, protocols, and everyday lives were in a constant state of flux. "A number of school leaders established 'check-in' protocols, where they made purposeful plans for regular contact with teachers, parents and students, particularly those who they felt were vulnerable or needed extra support to navigate the rapidly changing situation" (Longmuir, 2021, p. 9). The question was clear, how can principals ensure that they are reaching everyone throughout the school day without being physically present in the building?

During the age of virtual teaching, it was easy for a desktop screen to quickly become overcrowded with video conferencing windows, documents, and files. Most days, my screen was drowning in browser tabs, and my inbox overflowed from the more than normal emails being sent. Due to the fact that protocols and procedures were in a continuous state of change, administrators updated teachers and staff hourly. Longmuir (2021) notes:

> School leaders described how they had to abandon their normal consultative processes and procedures of seeking input and advice during a major change in favor of independent decisiveness and implementing the best solution most quickly. Information changed rapidly and there was a significant sense of urgency to implement responses. (p. 9)

However, it became clear that as a teacher, it was unfeasible to monitor the constant flow of important information via email while also focusing on instruction. In order to alleviate teachers from the burden of emails while remaining connected with staff, my principal creatively solved this problem by making use of a shared document. All staff were given access to the document, and the title "Remote Learning—Live Updates" was fittingly given. This became our staff's home base for the rest of the time we were teaching virtually from home.

This document allowed teachers to easily keep in touch with one another, ask questions, share resources, and find updated information instantly without being hit with a tsunami of emails. The page was separated into four sections, date, information, teacher feedback/questions, and answers. Staff was freely given permission to edit and update the document whenever they had a question, concern, or share resources. In my opinion, the true innovation and originality came with the system's ease of use and simplicity. All relevant information was stored in an easily accessible location instead of being buried in the depths of an email chain. Before the school year's end, we had filled almost fifty full pages with writing, pictures, links, and videos. Along the way, many teachers and our principal used it to show gratitude for one another, express daily struggles, and celebrate personal and educational wins. Teachers used it to socially interact with grade-level teams, colleagues, and friends. While at this point in the pandemic, it may seem like second nature for school leaders to take advantage of such communication strategies, in my experience, this was not a traditional means of transmitting and receiving information for principals prior.

> To provide this information, principals frequently tapped into existing communication infrastructures, such as automated phone

calls, text messages, or weekly email newsletters. For many, however, this infrastructure was insufficient, so they increased both the frequency of communications and the methods they used to communicate and involved other staff to help reach students and families. (Kaul et al., 2020, p. 4)

While a shared document is just one example of how communication was established, principals had little choice but to expand upon their traditional communication modalities and find alternative methods.

Staff Appreciation

With the end of the year looming on the horizon and staff morale at an all-time low, teachers were in dire need of relief from the daily disruptions that coincided with COVID-19. Being forced to deliver all instruction virtually, in the middle of the year, without any notice, took a toll on all staff members' emotional and mental health. "School closures and the pivot to distance learning came with increased workloads and difficulties in the transition to working from home" (Baker et al., 2021). Speaking personally, my own level of emotional distress was increasing daily and the terms and conditions of remote teaching sparked feelings of anxiety and inadequacy. Baker et al. (2021) explains, "The findings suggest, unsurprisingly, that experiencing more stressors was associated with worse self-reported mental health and with finding it 'harder to cope' and 'harder to teach.'" It's hard to imagine that what started as a short-term two-week school closure out of an abundance of caution had now turned into a full-blown catastrophe with no light at the end of the tunnel. When the situation seemed most grim, I can vividly recall my principal showing his appreciation for the dedication and resilience of the staff in a special way.

After logging into our last staff meeting of the year, I watched the small squares of my colleagues appear on the screen one by one. Even after weeks of virtual meetings, it still felt strange to see teachers' faces in their living rooms, kitchens, backyards, and driving in cars. Once everyone was accounted for, my principal started the meeting by reviewing end-of-the-year procedures. The meeting continued normally as we reviewed the items of the agenda. Once at the end of the meeting, my principal paused, took a deep breath, and changed tone.

> I know this year has been unlike any other, but it has been an extreme privilege to work alongside you all as we navigate the ups and downs of the situation. I wrote a story to show my appreciation for everything you have done for our school and students. It's called *"The Little School That Could"* and is about all we have experienced during the last few months.

At this point, he held up what appeared to be a hardcover book that prominently featured a beautiful picture of our 1920s school building on its cover. He went on to tell a story depicting the school's transformation from the time he started his principalship. It described how, "*Extra help, clubs, parent support, innovative lessons and creative planning and scheduling really took kids' efforts and achievement to higher and higher levels!*" The story highlighted the unique ways each individual, from teachers to lunch aides, helps students reach their goals each and every day. However, the story turned when "*Everyone in the land was getting sick. The halls were empty, and kids had to learn from home. This situation was very difficult for everyone and the staff faced yet another challenge that they needed to solve.*" It went on to recognize that despite the hardships brought on by the pandemic, "*The Little School That Could*" just changed paths and forged ahead. "*There were flip grids, virtual scavenger hunts, live meetings with entire classes, and virtual class trips! The Staff even planned a car parade with cheers and honks! All the while, they spent much time and effort trying and trying to find ways to help kids learn without even being in the classroom!*"

My principal read the book as he beamed with genuine pride for us and what we accomplished in the face of extreme adversity.

With the theme of staff appreciation in mind, effective leaders will need to continue demonstrating a sense of caring and compassion through their communications to support all members of the school community.

> The overarching sense of the importance of a caring, compassionate approach to leading showed that, at a time of crisis, leaders return to the humanising purposes of education. They focused on the foundational needs of all members of the community and ensured that these were prioritised before any organizational or learning requirements. (Longmuir, 2021, p. 11)

The reading of "The Little School That Could" did not resolve the large systemic issues we were facing as teachers, but it did make me feel like a valued and appreciated member of my school community.

Similarly, it is also relevant to explore the process of returning to in-person learning and how it relates to staff appreciation. While the ordeal of returning to in-person learning throughout the pandemic is a saga in and of itself, the main issue in our district quickly became staffing. "A dearth of day-to-day and long-term substitutes to fill in for teachers on extended leaves of absence means, in some districts, teachers have to cover classes for their absent colleagues" (Carver-Thomas et al., 2021). With nearly no substitutes due to the high risks of COVID-19, when teachers were required to quarantine, non-grade level-specific teachers were pulled from their duties to cover classes throughout the building. This arrangement was inconvenient for all involved; however, it was the only way for our school to remain open for our students. Special area classes (art, music, basic skills) would be canceled, and classroom teachers would have to do without any planning periods throughout the day. Inevitably this led to a massive feeling of fatigue and frustration in all of our building staff. Even halfway through the 2021–2022 school year, my colleagues and I occasionally get asked to fill in for classes if we are understaffed on a particular day.

While I can't recall any specific moment or example, I do always remember feeling appreciated and well respected by my school administrators through their words and actions. They checked in with teachers regularly, asked if they needed breaks, and always made sure to express gratitude through verbal and written communications. This type of genuine acknowledgment and recognition went a long way and allowed me to personally overcome my frustrations in regards to the circumstances to do what was best for our students and school. On a side note, I would like to add that being a substitute in a variety of grade levels allowed me to see our school through the lens of a classroom teacher. This would have been impossible had it not been for the pandemic. As someone who is not a grade-level teacher, this was a huge learning experience and exposed me to resources, pedagogy, and instruction that I would have otherwise missed as an aspiring school leader. I highly recommend all aspiring leaders make their best efforts to habitually observe, teach, and, if possible, substitute for a class outside their area of expertise.

Conclusion

As the pandemic continues to linger, it is undeniable that both educators and school leaders will be responding to the fallout of COVID-19 for years to come. In her 2021 inaugural poem "The Hill We Climb," Amanda Gorman speaks about the status of the United States in the midst of arguably one of the largest national crises of our generation. "So, while once we asked, how could we possibly prevail over catastrophe, now we assert, how could catastrophe possibly prevail over us" (Gorman, 2021, p. 209)? While Gorman is speaking about the nation as a whole, I think the sentiment can be shared to education. As we learn to live with COVID-19, humanity will need to continually overcome the virus's struggles derived, both indirectly and directly. But now that we are learning to adjust and refocus in all facets of society, I think it's prudent that we continually ask ourselves, are we going to allow adversity to stop us from reaching the top of the hills we climb as aspiring leaders?

With the future of education in an unpredictable state, current aspiring school administrators can prepare to lead by observing the behaviors and actions of those currently experiencing the pandemic in real-time.

Observational learning will present developing leaders with a roadmap, or general sense, on what to expect post COVID-19, how to handle situations, or possibly what to avoid when making decisions. On its own, observational learning won't be enough to fill every bucket for future leaders, but it is a good place to start. Given the current climate of education, your role as a future leader is more important now than ever. It is my hope that by reflecting on past practices and considering the fusion of leadership practices currently being utilized, the next generation of school leaders can continue to grow in order to engineer unique approaches of their own. In turn, building schools that are more resilient for the future.

REFERENCES

Bagwell, J. (2020). Leading Through a Pandemic: Adaptive Leadership and Purposeful Action. *Journal of School Administration Research and Development*, 5(S1), 30–34. https://doi.org/10.32674/jsard.v5is1.2781

Baker, C. N., Peele, H., Daniels, M., Saybe, M., Whalen, K., & Overstreet, S. (2021). The experience of COVID-19 and its impact on teachers' mental health, coping, and teaching. *School Psychology Review*, 50(4), 491–504. https://doi.org/10.1080/2372966X.2020.1855473

Bandura, A. (1977). Self-efficacy: Toward a unifying theory of behavioral change. *Psychological Review*, 84(2), 191–215. https://doi.org/10.1037/0033-295X.84.2.191

Bandura, A. (1986). *Social foundations of thought and action*. Prentice-Hall.

Bandura, A. (1994). Self-efficacy. In V. S. Ramachaudran (Ed.), *Encyclopedia of human behavior* (Vol. 4, pp. 71–81). Academic Press. (Reprinted in H. Friedman [Ed.], *Encyclopedia of mental health*. San Diego: Academic Press, 1998).

Bandura, A. (1999). Social cognitive theory: An agentic perspective. *Asian Journal of Social Psychology*, 9, 21–41.

Brion, C. (2021). Creating intentionally inviting school cultures. *Journal of Interdisciplinary Studies in Education*, 10(1), 160–181.

Carver-Thomas, D., Leung, M., & Burns, D. (2021). California teachers and COVID-19: How the pandemic is impacting the teacher workforce. *Learning Policy Institute*.

Gorman, A. (2021). The hill we climb. In *Call us what we carry: Poems*. Viking Books.

Groenendijk, T., Janssen, T., Rijlaarsdam, G., & van den Bergh, H. (2013). The effect of observational learning on students' performance, processes, and motivation in two creative domains. *The British journal of educational psychology*, 83(1), 3–28. https://doi.org/10.1111/j.2044-8279.2011.02052.x

Grusec, J. E. (1992). Social learning theory and developmental psychology: The legacies of Robert Sears and Albert Bandura. *Developmental Psychology*, 28(5), 776–786.

Harris, A., & Jones, M. (2020). COVID 19—School leadership in disruptive times. *School Leadership & Management*, 40(4), 243–247. chttps://doi.org/10.1080/13632434.2020.1811479

Kaul, M., VanGronigen, B. A., Simon, N. S., & University of Pennsylvania, C. for P. R. in E. (CPRE). (2020). *Calm during Crisis: School principal approaches to crisis management during the COVID-19 pandemic. Leading in Crisis. Research Brief.* Consortium for Policy Research in Education.

Kempster, S. (2009). Observing the invisible: Examining the role of observational learning in the development of leadership practice. *The Journal of Management Development, 28*(5), 439–456. https://doi.org/10.1108/02621710910955976

Longmuir, F. (2021). *Leading in lockdown: Community, communication and compassion in response to the COVID-19 crisis.* Educational Management Administration & Leadership. https://doi.org/10.1177/17411432211027634

Maloney, T., & Garver, R. (2020). Preparing Future School Leaders: Pre-service School Leaders' Sensemaking of Supervising for Equity. *Journal of Education Human Resources, 38*(1), 82–105.

Myers, C. G. (2020). Vicarious learning in the time of coronavirus. *Behavioral Science & Policy 6*(2), 153–161. https://doi.org/ 10.1353/bsp.2020.0026.

Pawlas, G .E. (2005). *Administrator's guide to school-community relations* (2nd ed.). Routledge. https://doi.org/10.4324/9781315853673

Voight, A., Austin, G., & Hanson, T. (2013). *A climate for academic success: How school climate distinguishes schools that are beating the achievement odds* (Full Report). WestEd.

Weiner, J., Francois, C., Stone-Johnson, C., & Childs, J. (2021). Keep safe, keep learning: principals' role in creating psychological safety and organizational learning during the COVID-19 pandemic. *Frontiers in Education, 5*, 282. https://doi.org/10.3389/feduc.2020.618483

CHAPTER 6

TEACHER BURNOUT + YOU

What Can You Do?

Brenda Lisette Chavez

Beginning in January 2020, across the United States news started to spread about a contagious illness called COVID-19. Everyone took the news differently. Some people started to get worried, others waited to see what would happen. Some parents even started sending their children with masks and gloves to school. It seemed unusual and maybe even laughable at the time, but little did we know that it would get very serious, very soon. By March 2020, COVID-19 was declared a Public Health Emergency. COVID-19 slowly worked its way into becoming a pandemic. Many teachers across New Jersey were told that they would be teaching virtually for at least a week. In my district, it was one week of virtual with Spring break coming soon. I remember hearing all the chatter about what was going to happen. No one knew what the future would hold. No one knew that one week would quickly become more than two years of teaching virtually. Districts tried their best to give teachers professional development right before going virtual so that they would feel ready to embark upon this new journey. I remember sitting at a professional development training feeling hopeful. My district really tried everything in their power to make sure that we felt confident going into this uncharted territory. I felt confident that I would be able to do what they asked of me. Unfortunately, I knew that was not the case for all the teachers. I made myself available to my colleagues in case they needed help. I remember being at that professional development training where they showed us all these cool websites that we could use with our students and seeing some of my coworkers feeling a little weary. Through it all, I must say that I did feel a little bit of excitement. I was excited to try the new technology and to be home. It would be nice not to have to wake up so early and rush to school. What started as a fun, technologically innovative way to teach, quickly changed into something else completely. It started to feel like a nightmare that you could not wake up from. "COVID-19 created unprecedented challenges for schools, staff, and students" (Dabrowski, 2020, p. 4).

One of the challenges that the pandemic created was that it made it difficult for educators to keep boundaries. When did work start and when did work end? Should I answer this message even though it is late? What more can I do to help my students? These were all questions that would run through my head the whole time I was teaching virtually. Now that we are living in a post-pandemic world, what can current and future leaders do to help ease teachers and prevent them from burning out? Social-emotional well-being is important for students, but who asks teachers how they are doing? And when asking teachers how they are feeling, is social-emotional well-being even taken into consideration? What can you do to make teacher well-being a priority? How can morale be boosted in a school where spirits are low? This chapter will explore ways that current and future administrators can be there for their staff through traumatic events and through tough times.

One of the biggest difficulties with teaching virtually was teachers losing boundaries. When you are teaching in person at your school with all your students, things are different. You have communication with your parents, but there are boundaries. Parents know that you will not always get to their messages during school time because you are in the middle of teaching. Parents are a little more respectful about response times. Parents also know that when you are home those replies may be delayed as well. When you are teaching in person, you also have a choice of staying after 3 P.M. or going home right away. It is your choice when you choose to leave the school building. Leaving at contractual hours does not mean that all your teacher duties are completely finished. Teachers must grade assignments, create plans, and communicate with parents. One way to establish boundaries is by limiting the amount of time you spend doing those things. The workload will never end, but you can control how much of your time you are giving up. Your workspace is independent of your living space. During virtual teaching, teachers were accessible at all hours. Administrators were available too, but teachers felt the bulk of the work. We were the ones communicating with our students and our parents. We were the ones that had to face our students. When you finished grading a bunch of virtual assignments, new ones would be turned in. You would also have to prepare for virtual teaching the next day. Work did not seem to finish. It seemed to go on forever and then the same thing would be repeated the next day. It felt like the movie *Groundhog Day* except nothing got better by changing your decisions, you had the same ending every time.

LESSONS LEARNED

Boundaries

I will never forget my first day of virtual teaching. I remember the night before I made sure that my computer was fully charged. I woke up extra early in case I had to troubleshoot and help my students. I was so nervous about what would happen to my students with them being home. I knew it was not exactly equitable, but this was the only way we could all be safe for the time being. I was afraid that some students would not be able to complete the tasks at hand. At the time we did not have one-to-one technology yet. My district began virtual teaching by using a video program called Flipgrid. On the first day at 8:00 A.M., I kept refreshing Flipgrid waiting to see a student's video. Finally, after refreshing for over 20 minutes, I saw my first student's video. I felt so happy, and I sent that student video feedback. I spent my first two hours of the day just watching videos and giving video feedback. There was a point in the day when I did not receive any more videos. Then late at night, students that did not participate throughout the day did. That first day was just a little taste of what was to come. I remember staying up at all hours responding back with a video to my students. I graded the videos and made sure to provide meaningful feedback. As late as 10 P.M., I would have students still submitting work. I felt that it was my duty to get back to them and that if I did not respond, I would be failing them. I used Flipgrid for about two weeks until my district introduced us to a new program called Zoom. At first, Zoom was incredible because I could communicate with my students in real-time. At that point, all my students had a device to use and had free internet access. My district did a wonderful job trying to make sure that all students could learn.

I remember seeing their little boxes and it felt like we were in person. I got a glimpse of what their life was like at home, and they got to see mine. I saw their pets roaming around in the background. I heard their siblings learning how to read in their own "class." When I started virtual teaching, I started in my living room, but with my two siblings being virtual too, it meant that I would have to find a better space. I ended up teaching in my bedroom for over two years. The same place I would sleep in became my classroom. It was not the most ideal situation, and it was the situation for not only me but for many others. It was difficult to separate work life and home life by that point. Zoom really was a gamechanger because we could share our screens and we could communicate through chat. These features made teaching a bit easier. Zoom was not exactly like being in the classroom, but it was a huge upgrade from using Flipgrid. Everything was not all sunshine and rainbows though. There were many technical difficulties and many students had issues with using Zoom. Zoom would go down and lag. It would also randomly kick out students. Days like that meant that many messages had to be sent to parents on ClassDojo explaining the situation and the steps that had to be taken to fix the issue. After our Zoom sessions, I would create videos to help them with their math work, and then I had to watch their Flipgrid exit videos. I would be on my computer almost all day except for when I would eat. My eyes would be so tired at the end of the night before I would go to bed. The communication that I had with my family was nonstop. I would be talking to them from the moment I woke up until I went to bed. I was in a constant state of exhaustion because I did not know where to draw the line. It felt like there was no excuse for me to not answer because I was home, and I could easily respond. I just wanted to help no matter the cost. It is not surprising that I wasn't the only one that did not know how to establish boundaries. Many of my coworkers were also up at all hours. My administrators were great and would tell us to take it easy. They acknowledged our hard work and were thankful for all that we were doing, but we did not stop or take a break. It is not their fault that we felt the need to keep going, to keep pushing our students so that they could be successful. We just wanted our students to feel as close to being in the classroom as possible and to be able to help them. Teachers want what is best for their students and that is exactly what we were trying to do.

As a future administrator, I would make it clear to my staff that is very important to have that line of communication open with parents, but boundaries are also very important. I wish someone would have told me that although I wanted to be helpful and present, I needed to create boundaries. If I didn't create those boundaries for myself, I would feel drained all the time. I remember "Zooming" in the morning, watching and responding to videos, communicating with parents, and then going to graduate English as a Second Language (ESL) and BL classes myself. On top of everything, I was also creating slides that would make my teaching the next day easier. I started to lose myself and my family started to notice. I am upbeat and happy, but I was starting to feel sad and not like myself. Even the things that used to bring me so much joy did not anymore because I was always thinking what if that one student needed help or if I should be making a video so that I could help my students. I was juggling so many things that there really wasn't time to do the things I liked. This was the sad reality for many teachers. They worked nonstop and their well-being started to decline. Harris and Jones (2020) suggest that self-care should be a priority in schools.

Another difficulty that educators faced during the pandemic was how lonely virtual teaching was. When you are in school, there are plenty of opportunities for you to collaborate with your coworkers. You could pop into a colleague's room and share ideas; you could discuss ideas during lunch or even at dismissal. When you had professional development (PD) opportunities, it was another chance for you to talk to someone and see what was working in their classroom. Ideas were everywhere. Virtual learning made you feel like you were navigating the waters alone. I remember only seeing my colleagues during professional learning communities or PDs. I never got to interact with anyone else from my school at any other time during the day. I was lucky I lived with my family because if I did not, I probably wouldn't have spoken to anyone. We were all in our own little virtual world. My frustrations, my successes, and everything in-between were not shared with anyone. Throughout the time we were quarantined, my district gave us surveys in which they tried to check in with their staff. I know they gave us mental health resources and people we could contact if we wanted to talk to someone. I feel like that was a great idea and it might have helped many teachers that were struggling. School-based administrators gave support, but this also teaches us a lesson if virtual teaching ever happens again. Administrators must check in with their staff. You must build trust and relationships so they can express these types of concerns. As a teacher, I do daily check-ins with my students to gauge how they are feeling. You can do that with your staff as well. As an administrator, you can pop in just to see how they are doing. Building relationships is just asking how are you doing? You will get a generic answer like "I'm good." You need to dive deeper and ask more thought-provoking questions. An example of this is asking "Is there anything I could do to help you" or "how could you feel better supported?" These types of questions will probably give you a better response. Another solution could be professional learning networks (PLNs), which could facilitate communication and help your staff feel less alone. If these steps are taken early, I believe it will help alleviate some of the loneliness that comes with being virtual.

Coping With Stressful Events

Wang et al. (2022) looked at coping strategies that Canadian teachers used. They understood that teachers have many different coping strategies that they need to maintain their well-being. What was interesting about the approach that they used was that they used a person-centered approach. A person-centered approach is when you "assume that the population is heterogeneous concerning the relations between the predictors and the outcomes" (p. 3). What their study found was that problem-focused coping yielded better results for teachers because they felt more positive emotions. All this means is that teachers tend to cope by solving a problem head-on rather than disengage. Social support is also useful for their well-being. Teachers use a variety of coping strategies. Future and current leaders should identify the ways that their teachers cope with issues so that way they can assist when needed.

A study was done by Nabe-Nielson et al. (2021) in which they investigated how teachers from Denmark reacted to different phases of the COVID-19 pandemic. They looked at how their mental health changed throughout the pandemic. Their study was done in the form of a survey that asked questions such as how old they were, who they lived with, what grades they taught, and how they were expected to teach. Although my district was virtual for a very long time, other districts and countries were not the same. In this case, Denmark and other regions had teachers teaching in schools, remotely from home, and hybrid, Nabe-Nielson et al. also asked their participants if they belonged to an at-risk group for COVID-19. What this study found was that those teachers that belonged to the at-risk group had more emotional reactions. Teachers that were in the non-risk group worried about working conditions. Both groups had poor mental health. What does this mean for us, aspiring leaders? After such a traumatic event, I do think that teachers should have someone to talk to. Nabe-Nielson suggested that "extra resources should be given to teachers so that they could help students catch up on deficiencies" (p. 9). I do believe that having extra resources like counseling could help students thrive. Many students have not been in school for a very long time and even though they were learning virtually, they had to jump over many hoops to even just do that. Each school should have more than one social worker. We are trying to make it seem like life is back to normal. For a lot of teachers and students alike, things aren't the way that they were. Many students and teachers experienced loss. Their emotions have been like a roller coaster because there were moments of happiness and moments of sadness. It is very important to find someone to talk to after such an event as this, which is why more mental health resources need to be made available for all. Also, if teachers are feeling worried, a leader would reassure them and communicate so that they feel less worried.

The Importance of Leadership Style When Boosting School Morale

Even before the pandemic had started, I was attending graduate school in order to obtain my ESL and bilingual certifications from New Jersey City

University. Right before the pandemic began, I thought it would be a great idea to get my master's in educational leadership as well. I applied and got into Montclair's Educational Leadership Fast Track Program. The Educational Leadership Program was insightful. All throughout the graduate program, there has always been an emphasis on being good at communication. Professors have emphasized the importance of taking a few minutes out of your day to talk to your staff, students, parents, and community. In one graduate class, in particular, we explored and analyzed Lincoln's leadership. We then thought about how those ideals could be applied to our own leadership. As future leaders, we need to try and establish those relationships with our staff so that they feel comfortable enough to talk to us when they need to. That professor in particular talked about how taking five minutes to talk to someone will create a bond. Leaders need to build relationships; they will not be built on their own. Without those meaningful relationships, your staff will not express how they feel. I remember feeling like I was alone navigating the waters at some point, and I never wanted anyone to feel like that. I will always keep that in mind. You never know what someone is going through, the only way you will come close to knowing is by asking them and listening. I know that the situation we were in was unlike any other, and there were no handbooks that said this is what you should do, but teachers and students need reassurance. Both teachers and students need someone with a plan. They need to know that someone is there to support them and help them. Teachers should not have to say I need help all the time. As a leader, you should swoop before teachers get to that breaking point. That could mean joining the Zoom, taking over the class so that the teacher could take a few minutes to themselves.

One of the most important things that an administrator can do is familiarize themselves with the technology and curriculum. Harris and Jones (2020, p. 2) state that "school leaders will increasingly need to be technologically savvy and well informed." Although, as an administrator, you are not teaching a class, you should know what students are learning and need. Knowing the technology well makes it easier for you to help a teacher when they need to. You could just swoop in and help or even advise them with your knowledge. Future and current leaders should continuously research and be in the know. A perfect example of this was when I was in middle school, I had an amazing principal who knew the ins and outs of the school. He knew everyone by name, he would come in to teach us and give the teacher a break so that they could do other things. He was visible and supportive of his school. You looked forward to going to school because you knew he would be there. By him coming to teach us, he helped the teacher feel supported, and heard. He also alleviated some of the burdens the teachers had, so they did not burn out as quickly. This could only happen because he understood the balance "between technology and pedagogy" (Harris & Jones, 2020, p. 2).

I believe that one of the hardest things to do in a school after such a traumatic event as the COVID-19 pandemic is uniting it. As funny as it sounds, I was quite shy when we got back in person for hybrid learning in the spring of 2021. There were many restrictions still in place and you could not eat with other people in your room and so collaboration still did not exist in person. I even had a hard time talking to some of my friends. By the fall of 2021, we were all back in-person teaching full-time, and it took some time to adjust. I know I felt awkward at first because I was home with just my family and had not really seen my colleagues in such a long time. The thoughts that I had in my head were what do I say to them? Even having a whole class in person felt like a huge adjustment. I know my students felt it too. They did not know how to act and what was and was not allowed. My administrator did have faculty meetings with our whole school virtually and she tried her best to get us acclimated again, but it did take some time. As a future leader, I think that boosting a school's morale is one of the top things that should be done in a school. There were weekly spirit days on Friday where we could wear a certain shirt for the holiday that was coming up. This really helped unify us because we all felt like we were a part of the school. I remember looking to see which shirt color everyone had picked; it was nice to be unified. Having school spirit days also was one less decision that we teachers had to make. We knew that on Fridays we could wear that shirt, I did not have to look in my closet for something specific to wear. We were also given breakfast, which cheered us up. There was one teacher in our school that treated us to bagels. They kept announcing that on this particular day we would be getting breakfast from her. When the day came, we all went to get our bagels and it almost felt like old times. My principal provided us with room service after Back-to-School Night and Parent's Night. Something as simple as that made us feel better. You cannot go wrong with giving teachers and staff a free breakfast or lunch. Again, part of the reason why this works is because it is one less thing on your plate. As a teacher, you are constantly making decisions. I know from the moment I wake up to the time I go to bed, I am thinking of the next day or the day to come. By providing us with a meal, that is something I do not have to plan for, and it gives us extra time. I know that for budgetary reasons free breakfast and lunch cannot happen every day, but a monthly breakfast or lunch will get your morale up.

Most recently, our art teacher had students write love notes to teachers and she displayed them in common areas that teachers would go to. This simple project held a lot of meaning. Teachers would smile and point to their love notes and feel seen by their students. This is what is needed, small acts of kindness. Many times, teachers feel like they are being overlooked or that their work is not enough. These simple gestures help teachers' well-being and make them smile. I know I was happy and excited to find notes.

Before becoming an administrator, you are told to think about the type of leader that you want to be. Everyone has a leader that they admire, and that leader can even be the one that is in your building. Why do you admire them? One of the reasons you admire them is because of how they handle situations, or it can be because of their leadership style. Administrators must decide what their leadership style will be like. This decision will affect the school culture, teachers, students, and everything in a school. Kwatubana and Molaodi (2021) looked at leadership styles that would support teachers' well-being in Africa during the COVID-19 pandemic. They point out how critical teacher well-being is because it not only affects productivity, but it also affects student success. If a teacher is not satisfied and is feeling overworked and exhausted, then that leads to burnout. Burnout then leads to teachers leaving and that negatively impacts on a school. As an administrator, you want to keep your teachers happy, and you want them to stay. The solution always seems to point to teacher self-care, but administrators should take responsibility too. Kwatubana and Molaodi (2021) talk about the importance of planning. Future leaders, such as myself, should always have a plan. I know that as a teacher I have not only Plan B, but Plan C, D, E, and the list goes on. Harris and Jones (2020, p. 2) also state that "crisis and change management are necessary skills that a school leader should have. They should also have a high degree of trust." This goes back to establishing those connections. Administrators should also emphasize the importance of PLN teams. I know that during the pandemic, I worked alone most of the time. It would have been great to work in a PLN team because it would have alleviated a lot of the stress I felt. I am sure other teachers would have appreciated it too. It is not that we were told we shouldn't work together, but there were not opportunities to get together to bring this issue up.

We should be compassionate leaders, which means we should not be quick to judge or act. In fact, Kwatubana and Molaodi (2021) state that compassionate leadership means "being in contact with your staff, actively listening without judgment and assisting when necessary" (p. 5). It is important to be a good listener because if you do not you will never know what the other person is going through. I feel that COVID-19 made us more compassionate with each other because it changed our mentality from not caring to caring. After all, you never know what might happen. When we take a few moments to listen, we become empathetic, and that trust is made stronger. Compassion and emotional support are important keys to being a successful leader.

Research on leadership style consistently shows that leaders that have a transformational approach are more effective. Masry-Herzallah and Stavissky (2021, p. 3) looked at the effect of transformational leadership and a school's success during virtual learning. Some of the qualities that transformational leaders have include recognizing the success and achievements of others, positively influencing their teachers, and transmitting their school's mission by modeling it. Masry-Herzallah and Stavissky found that transformational leaders did in fact communicate better with their staff and helped made online learning a success. This was not the only study that has looked at transformational leadership, Tsang et al. (2022) explored the relationship between transformational leadership and teacher burnout. Tsang et al. define burnout as an "individuals' personal stress in long-term jobs. It is comprised of three dimensions, which include emotional exhaustion, depersonalization, and reduced personal accomplishment" (p. 2). For teachers, it is evident that during the pandemic many felt emotional exhaustion as well as physical exhaustion. It is interesting to see that their study showed that transformational leadership helps prevent teacher burnout. This happens because teachers feel that their work is valued and meaningful. Lastly, Dabrowski (2020) suggested that administrators and leaders should "invite educators to be a part of the broader conversations so that everyone including students and parents can emerge from this crisis stronger" (p. 4). Teachers are usually put to the side, and no one really asks them their thoughts. When their thoughts are shared, they are usually ignored or laughed at. Teachers need to be taken seriously and recognized for all that they do.

Learning From the Past

As cheesy as it sounds, we need to learn from our past and from the experiences that have happened to us. Like Kwatubana and Molaodi (2021) stated is important to listen to our teachers and students. Communication between all parties must continue. Teachers and school leaders alike need to partake in self-care (Harris & Jones, 2020). Without self-care and establishing boundaries, it will lead to burnout, which is something that could be avoided with the proper tools and help. A school leader needs to also be aware of the technology and curriculum in their school. Administrators that know the ins and outs of a school so that they are the best leaders. This also means that they will be ready to help when needed. For example, as an administrator, you should be able to troubleshoot when using Zoom. You should be aware of the different applications and technology that are used in the classroom. It seems trivial, but if you walk into a classroom and do not know how to help a teacher, then you should get a refresher. It is important to be a part of professional development. This not only helps with the school's mission and vision, but you will be a supportive leader. Tsang et al. (2022, p. 8) also suggests that administrators should be good role models with clear visions. These visions need to be modeled and emphasized. Sharing the vision will help inspire teachers and make them feel like they are a part of something great. Administrators need to have plans that include teachers and make them feel valued because they are. Administrators can make teachers feel valued by asking for their input, writing thank you notes to show appreciation, and taking over their class occasionally. Teachers are crucial in schools and should be appreciated for all that they do for our children. Dabrowski (2020) realizes that teacher well-being is important too. Teachers are the center and base of the school, if they crumble, the school crumbles along with it. Leaders clearly need to look at their leadership style and if they are not currently transformational leaders that uplift their teachers then they need to work on that. New aspiring leaders have the chance to make a change and make teachers aware of how great they are. Teacher burnout, leadership style, and teacher well-being are all interconnected, and they all start with you. You be the change and be what makes teachers feel empowered. We can learn so much from the pandemic. We can learn how to be better and how to be compassionate because what is life without caring for one another? We are the future of education, let's make it brighter for everyone.

REFERENCES

Dabrowski. A., (2020). Teacher wellbeing during a pandemic: Surviving or thriving? *Social Education Research, 2*(1), 35–40. https://doi.org/10.37256/ser.212021588

Harris, A., & Jones, M. (2020). Covid 19—School leadership in disruptive times. *School Leadership & Management, 40*(4), 243–247. https://doi.org/10.1080/13632434.2020.1811479

Kwatubana, S., & Molaodi, V. (2021). *Leadership styles that would enable school leaders to support the wellbeing of teachers during COVID-19.* Bulgarian Comparative Education Society.

Masry-Herzallah, A., & Stavissky, Y. (2021). Investigation of the relationship between transformational leadership style and teachers' successful online teaching during Covid-19. *International Journal of Instruction, 14*(4), 891–912. https://doi.org/10.29333/iji.2021.14451a

Nabe-Nielsen, K., Christensen, K. B., Fuglsang, N. V., Larsen, I., & Nilsson, C. J. (2021). The effect of COVID-19 on schoolteachers' emotional reactions and mental health: longitudinal results from the CLASS study. *International Archives of Occupational & Environmental Health, 95,* 855–865. https://doi.org/10.1007/s00420-021-01806-8

Tsang, K. K., Du, Y., & Teng, Y. (2022). Transformational leadership, teacher burnout, and psychological empowerment: A mediation analysis. *Social Behavior and Personality: An International Journal, 50*(1), 1c. https://doi-org.ezproxy.montclair.edu/10.2224/sbp.11041

Wang, H., Lee, S. Y., & Hall, N. C. (2022). Coping profiles among teachers: Implications for emotions, job satisfaction, burnout, and quitting intentions. *Contemporary Educational Psychology, 68*. https://doi-org.ezproxy.montclair.edu/10.1016/j.cedpsych.2021.102030

CHAPTER 7

COLLABORATION

Joseph Cashin

"Mr. Cashin!", Shreya, one of my quieter students, shouted through the screen, "You're famous on TikTok!" My heart sank. I do not have a TikTok account. I will never have a TikTok account. I am a by-the-book English teacher at Thomas High School. My students know I care deeply about them, and I am not strict by any definition of the word, but they also know I am a buttoned-up professional. So who recorded me? I asked, "What do you mean?" Shreya responded, "Tell him Austin!" Austin is a kind, funny, and driven young man that did not care about English class. He held up his phone and explained that a TikTok he made had gone a little viral. With "Blue Blood" by Heinz Kiessling (a song used by the show *It's Always Sunny in Philadelphia*) playing in the background, the video flashes up my "assignment" from Google Classroom that asked the students to go outside and enjoy the warmer weather. The video then shows Austin's Minecraft player walking out of a house and enjoying the "great outdoors." The TikTok received over 175 thousand views. I am not sure if it is viral by 2022 standards, but we all had a good laugh about it during a time when everyone wanted to laugh more.

Later that day, another student named Rishita had a different reaction to the assignment. At the start of the pandemic the English Department got together, and we decided that one of our top priorities would be providing students with multiple avenues for students to contact us. Office hours, chat rooms, email hours, and ending class a few minutes early were all approaches we took to make ourselves available to our students. In my

---

Preparing to Lead:
Narratives of Aspiring School Leaders in a "Post"-COVID World, pp. 53–60
Copyright © 2024 by Information Age Publishing
www.infoagepub.com
All rights of reproduction in any form reserved.

classes, taking the time to share when we ended class early was the most beneficial window for my students. Rishita wanted to let me know she had not been allowed out of her room. Her family was so scared of coronavirus that they were not allowing each other to leave designated areas of their home. Immediately I thought, what could I do to help her? Unfortunately, there was nothing I could do to help.

The paranoia her family felt was not unfounded or uncommon for my school community at the start of the pandemic. At Thomas High School I am an English teacher in my seventh year. We are located in a major city in New Jersey, close to New York City. Our students have family members that work in Manhattan and family members that live in India. The borough of Manhattan and the country of India were two of the hardest-hit hotspots during the start of the pandemic. Our school was inundated with stories of family members losing jobs, family members falling ill, and family members passing away. It was a grim time for our school community, and the teachers focused on providing a positive distraction and supporting our learners. Even though I could not help Rishita leave her room, I was able to help other students through the decisions made with the input and support of my colleagues.

The most direct path we decided to take to support our students was using empathy. Through empathy, we were aware of and sensitive to the stresses that the pandemic had placed on our students. Empathy is a major component of educators across the country. Through building strong relationships with students and colleagues, we become empathy machines that can recognize when a student or colleague needs support, extra time, and/or extra space. During the pandemic, our empathy kicked into overdrive. The television and internet were full of stories of teachers, administrators, and other staff members helping students survive a deadly pandemic that was gripping the entire world.

I love the colleagues with whom I work in my department, and I would not have gotten through the height of the pandemic without them. The moment the pandemic hit, I knew I had a group of colleagues I could lean on for support, advice, and guidance. We would call, text, and video conference with each other before school, during our prep periods, and after school. It is not hyperbolic to say that I will remember the way we helped each other for the rest of my life. An example that stands out to me was when I met with the Graduation Portfolio teacher, Ms. Collins. The Graduation Portfolio class is a small section of students that need to pass College Board's ACCUPLACER test or create an English Portfolio of multiple essays in order to graduate. Ms. Collins and I share a few Seniors each year. During the pandemic, we shared a student named Aaliyah that was close to dropping out. Ms. Collins and I would meet a few times to see what approaches would work best for Aaliyah. Before the end of the winter,

Aaliyah finally passed the ACCUPLACER test, just before she needed to develop her portfolio, and she was on track to graduate. Ashanti graduated and she is now pursuing a career in culinary arts.

When I think about that time and stories like that, I feel terrible for the teachers that did not have a support system. What about teachers in my building (and across the country) that did not have a collaborative environment? It is my opinion that not all schools and departments have the camaraderie my department does. One teacher in my department agreed with me when they said, "It is great in my department. But I also think it is different by the department and some people like to work alone." And during a crisis, we all need community. As a future leader, I want to implement an environment where teachers have a colleague support system, regardless of building size. Isolation leads to burnout in an already depleted profession. It needs to be every administrator's responsibility to create and maintain environments that allow for collaboration between teachers.

Thomas High School Background

During the spring quarter of 2021, I added an extra class of Senior students for a colleague that was out on maternity leave. By the spring of 2021, New Jersey allowed each family to pick if they would like their student to Zoom into class or attend in-person. With a few students in-person and the majority online, I asked the seniors to share the colleges they would be attending in the fall. Meant as a celebration of their accomplishments, no one volunteered. I eventually had about 4 of the 30 students volunteer. As we wrapped up class early, I asked the in-person students why they thought no one wanted to share. They explained that their classmates were maybe embarrassed to share they would not be attending Harvard, Yale, or Princeton in the fall. Instead, they were attending Rutgers, the University of Michigan, and UCLA. Although upsetting to me and many other staff members, this mentality is not surprising.

Thomas High School has a history of being hyper-focused on academics. In 2016, the school was nicknamed "Billionaire High." In a news article, the former principal was quoted as saying, "The kids have the desire to succeed and be noticed. They don't want to settle for No. 2, No. 3, and *definitely* [sic] not No. 4. They want to be No. 1 and will push themselves." The intense drive of the student body and their families has resulted in high test scores, high graduation rates, high (elite-)college admissions, and high state rankings. Consistently ranked as one of the top 20 traditional public high schools in New Jersey (*U.S. News & World Report*, *Newsweek*, *Patch*, etc.), Thomas High School is also among the top five large-size traditional public high schools in New Jersey with enrollment above 2,500 students. "Bullying" at our high school often centers around the student's perceived intelligence and not always the traditional targets like looks or athletic ability. Bullying in academia is nothing new. Dentith et al. (2015) share their experiences of being mistreated because of their gender, age, and perceived intelligence even though they were colleagues with the same level of education. They reference being "belittled and talked to in a condescending manner" (p. 31). And the mistreatment was not always to their faces. Behind-the-scenes meetings were also places to put down the authors and one described hearing of a meeting where the atmosphere was " 'cutthroat,' [and] several present faculty ignored facts and preferred to spread unfounded rumor" (p. 32). These stories are near examples of situations we experience at Thomas High School. Too often, the students are picked on for doing well, but not the best of the best. Therefore, it was more understandable why my additional seniors did not want to share their college selections with the class.

This environment keeps teachers focused on their subject area to do the best job they possibly can. Teachers around the building have similar mindsets to one English teacher who noted, "The kids are high achieving. If they are going to work that hard, I can't fail them." Students walk into their high school experience with the expectation that they will be attending Princeton four years later. Many students begin studying for the SAT in middle school, many students join multiple clubs, and many students complete hours of community service each month. With the time and energy students put into their education process, some teachers feel they need to match that expectation. Just like our students, unobtainable goals are set, isolation sets inm and some teachers burn out or do not see the benefit of worrying about anything else outside of their classroom.

Teachers in Thomas High School are typically hyper-focused on their subject area, and they are often isolated by their subject-area department. Teachers are used to receiving multiple emails the moment a grade is posted to the online parent portal. During the pandemic, a Board of Education member openly questioned the Math Department's process and criticized them for not inputting grades in a timely manner during a public meeting. This causes faculty to watch their backs and worry about their classrooms. Go-to groups for teachers in my building is their department, and colleagues believe the strong collaboration that takes place in the building is only in their departments. Even a teacher from the smaller Business Department (of only three teachers) explained, "I believe that, as far as department-wise, the school does allow for departments to collaborate and form good relationships." However, that relationship-building does not extend to the entire school. I cannot remember speaking to a teacher outside of my subject area during the start of the pandemic. Throughout my interviews with teachers about Thomas High School's climate, they shared a love for their department but a detachment from the whole. One teacher perfectly outlined the belief that many hold: "In terms of the school-wide community, I feel that people in other departments barely know each other and barely want to, it is very compartmentalized." In addition, the same teacher followed up saying, "As a whole, I don't see [school-wide collaboration] as much. I think we are lacking a little bit, as far as faculty working together as a whole." In "normal times" that worked for some schools. Schools continue to support high-achieving students without school-wide collaboration. However, during the pandemic crisis, I saw the value of collaboration and I would like more administrators to support collaboration across the school.

English Department at Thomas High School

My department is fantastic, and I hope to use my supervisor's process as a guide when I become an educational leader. Our strong connections are founded on clear values set by the department chair. Collaboration with colleagues is one of those clear values. Three examples of activities related to collaboration include: our professional learning communities (PLC), our new-teacher induction, and our professional development.

Three Activities

First, we have strong grade-level PLC teams that are the base for the majority of our interactions. Grade-level teams are given authority to meet, discuss, and implement common assessments and adjustments to the curriculum. Instead of full-department meetings, we are often asked to meet with our grade-level teams instead. These meetings lead to friendships and collaborative partnerships. I know to reach out to my colleagues when I have a question or need advice and they know to reach out to me if they have a question or need advice.

Second, new teachers observe model teachers across the department, regardless of grade level. This provides the new teachers an opportunity to observe a variety of classroom management, lesson planning, and student engagement styles. Each half of the year the department supervisor reaches out to model teachers asking if they would be willing to open their classrooms to novice teachers. A schedule is set up and the novice teacher observes a lesson in a model teacher's classroom. The novice teacher is encouraged to walk around the classroom and ask the students questions. Conversations between the model teacher and novice teacher continue beyond the specific class period and the roles sometimes flip with the model teacher observing and providing feedback to the novice teacher.

Third, our teacher-led professional development takes priority over education companies. Colleagues are selected to teach about a range of topics from best practices to district initiatives. Our teacher-led professional development provides job-embedded learning that we find more valuable than hearing from an outsider. At the start of my career, the school district would spend big money to bring professional development companies in to share the latest and greatest innovations. To teachers across the country, it is no surprise that me and my colleagues did not find those sessions valuable. Instead, the teacher-led professional development we now engage with are quality sessions that we can use in our classrooms.

Unfortunately, not all departments have the same values. My department's focus on collaboration may not match other departments' focuses. Some are likely concerned with more traditionally individualized topics like test scores and implementing technology. A school leader needs to first be clear about their school's "shared understanding of and commitment to mission, vision, and core values within the school and the community" (Professional Standards for Educational Leaders 1f). In my view, a collaborative faculty is a central tenet. Aside from speaking it into existence, a school leader needs to be active to see collaboration in practice by completing walkthroughs and sitting in on department meetings. School leaders show the "value of particular reforms when they dedicate their own time to supporting those reforms rather than mainly outsourcing for support" (Honig & Rainey, 2019, p. 459). Implementing cross-curricular PLC teams is one way that can help move collaboration beyond specific departments. When staff members are confident that collaboration is valued, there is more buy-in to support the initiative. A school leader that dedicates their time to these initiatives needs to also follow through beyond the implementation stage.

Accountability

When a focus on collaboration is established, the school leader needs to hold teachers accountable. Our English department supervisor does a remarkable job of holding us accountable throughout the collaborative process. We are asked to submit reflections on the value and the opportunities for improvement before, during, and after our PLC meetings, induction support activities, and professional development sessions. We quickly understand that the work we do will be shared during future department meetings and professional development sessions. Through this process, we learn from each other. Leaders themselves learn through strong collaborative partnerships, that in some cases, span across buildings. Administrators improve when they see peers having success collaborating (Liou & Daly, 2020, p. 176). We become better educators when we understand that everyone has value. The educational leader needs to value all perspectives so that they can provide the best product for students (PSEL 3 c). Most educational leaders would agree that collaboration is necessary and beneficial. However, it only takes place with accountability.

Communication

Finally, a continuous step to improve collaboration is communication. In any strong administrative relationship, school leaders need to be focused on "articulating clear roles and expectations for both partners, [and] developing trust" (Thessin, 2019, p. 466). Trust was at the forefront during the pandemic. When the New Jersey state government sent out confusing decrees, teachers relied on building leadership to guide them. Clear communication saved valuable time for teachers. It also removed another potential frustration. There was no room for translating state directives on a to-do list that included learning how to video conference, recreating engaging lesson plans, and checking in on the well-being of one hundred students. The role of the administrator is to remove some of the obstacles for teachers so that they can better serve their students.

Conclusion

A few weeks after my TikTok fame, Rishita stayed after class again. She thanked me for listening and giving her the space to share what was bothering her. Although I could not help her, being there for her did the trick. But I would not have known that trick without the support of my English Department colleagues. Throughout my time at Thomas High School, they have shown themselves to be a reliable group that are aware of and sensitive to the highs and lows of teaching.

There is no doubt that establishing a collaborative environment is a difficult task for any leader to accomplish. But the pandemic taught us the need to have established support systems. I was very lucky. I feel terrible for the teachers that did not have a strong support system. Across the globe, people of all ages felt isolated at different times during the pandemic. Children could not see friends; adults could not see loved ones. In schools, teachers were responsible for more than just teaching. Schools that implemented processes before the crisis hit had a stronger environment for learning when the crisis hit. Once a crisis hits, it is too late. Rushed meetings that force people together feel disingenuous.

Beyond the pandemic, education leaders are faced with providing the best education for all learners. Collaboration allows teachers to feel supported, especially during difficult times. Both experienced and novice teachers can share experiences that can help future faculty and students. More importantly, collaboration leads to a safer environment with increased student achievement due to risk-taking and innovation. We feel terrible for the students that do not have access to safe environments, and across education school communities are focusing on establishing safer environments. When teachers are collaborative, they are stronger teachers. Students with better teachers have more access to better education. The educational leader should push beyond the difficulty of establishing a collaborative environment so that the school community can thrive before, during, and after a crisis.

REFERENCES

Dentith, A. M., Wright, R. R., & Coryell, J., (2015). Those mean girls and their friends: Bullying and mob rule in the academy. *Adult Learning, 26*(1), 28–34. http://dx.doi.org/10.1177/1045159514558409

Honig, M. I., & Rainey, L. R. (2019). Supporting principal supervisors: What really matters? *Journal of Educational Administration*.

Liou, Yi-Hwa, & Daly, A. J. (2020). The networked leader: understanding peer influence in a system-wide leadership team, *School Leadership & Management, 40*(2–3), 163–182. https://doi.org/10.1080/13632434.2019.1686611

Thessin, R. A. (2019). Establishing productive principal/principal supervisor partnerships for instructional leadership. *Journal of Educational Administration, 57*(5), 463–483. http://dx.doi.org/10.1108/JEA-09-2018-0184

CHAPTER 8

"BECAUSE IT'S EASY"

Lorin Hannah

Imagine growing up in Montana, going to college in Florida, and then becoming a teacher in New York City. Could you use your background as a farmer's kid to teach your students about wall street economics? Probably not. Sure, maybe you could relate selling tomatoes to stocks, but some might consider it a stretch. When you come from a state like New Jersey where the southern, middle, and northern parts of the state are like three different worlds, if you spend enough time in each of them you will find it difficult to feel at home anywhere. When I moved from my huge town in central Jersey with three high schools to a small farm town in South Jersey where I went to college, it was like I moved across the country. One day I was walking the halls with 1,500 other students all waiting for the final bell so we could get to the beach, meeting up with 3,000 of our closest friends from the other two high schools in our hometown. I think three people knew my name. Next thing I knew, I was looking for a parking spot in between a bunch of tractors, walking next to a thousand students that had no idea who I was, outside of the 50 or so students I had in class when I was a student teacher. Now, every Monday through Friday, I wake up in north Jersey, right outside of New York City and get ready for work. I walk two blocks down the street alongside 700 past, present, or future students. If I sneeze on my way to work, my neighbor, the superintendent, and at least 25 kids all say, "God bless you, Ms. Hannah."

It is hard to feel like you belong anywhere when everything feels out of place because you are so uncertain what will come next. Do not get me wrong, I love being in my classroom. The school where I work now *is* my home. Even though I knew this school would be my home from the moment I walked into my classroom for the very first time, something still did not feel right. But this was expected. When you are a first-year teacher everything is new and exciting. You are just trying to get through the year and navigate the workings of being a teacher. That feeling fades with time and experience, and you start to feel at home in your classroom, establishing expectations and procedures in compliance with school policy combined with your own morals and values. I was just starting to feel comfortable in my second year of teaching when the COVID-19 crisis hit. On March 16, 2020, Governor Phil Murphy announced that all schools would be closing in two days due to the increasing number of coronavirus cases. I walked home from work for the final time in the next two years. When I sneezed, no one said "God bless you." Or maybe they did, but I could not hear them because they all had a mask on.

When the pandemic first hit people were afraid to do anything. Prices were lower than ever on everything (except toilet paper) and the few willing to brave the outdoors could go and potentially pick up anything they wanted at an all-time low price. Non-essential businesses were practically giving things away. This, I thought, was short term. This would never last. While it may affect the economy for a short period of time, it would never get to larger industries, and it certainly would not have a lasting impact on education … or so I thought.

When we first went home, I had a total breakdown. I was in yet another unfamiliar place and the way I viewed schools changed again within such a short period of time. Everything I once knew was thrown out the window again and I had to start over. I was alone in my apartment with two cats and a computer screen. What I thought would last for two weeks lasted for two years and I hated every minute of it. Sure, my colleagues and I tried to make the best of a bad situation and did everything we could to innovate our lessons and make online school fun. But let's face it, online school was never fun. Teachers hated it. Kids hated it. I was frustrated by the way things happened. I was scared and angry. I did not want to be home. I wanted to be there for my kids. Being there for my kids was the one thing I could do whether I was volunteering to work with students with special needs in my high school, fitting into someone else's school and classroom as a student teacher or staying outside of my own classroom in the hallway for a few extra minutes just in case one of my students needed to drop by to talk. I began to think about ways to support my students from home. Although frustrated, I still loved the challenge.

One of my colleagues, a science teacher down the hall, started teaching the same year as me. Somewhere between attending football games, new teacher meetings, and fighting to get to the third-floor faculty bathroom first, we became close friends. We shared a passion for our students and our school, and the well-being of each and every one of the kids that walked into our classrooms. One day, when I was expressing my frustrations about online school to her, we totally lost it. We talked for hours about how we knew our kids were suffering and how we felt that there was not a thing we could do about it. As a social studies teacher, I began to think about different crises in the past and how famous world leaders handled them. I brought up President Franklin Delano Roosevelt and his "fireside chats," a series of radio broadcasts given to the people of the United States during difficult times. Hearing the president's voice over the radio brought the American people comfort and ensured them that everything was going to be okay. The high school we work at, known as the "Blue Tide" fit right into our theme and the "FireTide chats" were born. We started creating promotions to put on our school's social media page and the "walls" of our virtual classrooms and then every night around 5 o'clock we would sign on and just sit and talk with any student, parent, or teacher that either needed a safe space or wanted to help provide one for others. Some evenings we sat with a bunch of students for an hour or two and sometimes we stayed with a colleague that just needed to talk. Either way, we created something special. We were making a difference. Even when it seemed like we would be back in school soon and no one was logging on, I made sure to turn on my computer and sit there, just in case. I felt responsible for my students, my colleagues, and my parents. For the first time, I felt responsible for my school.

One pandemic Wednesday, we were scheduled to have a Parent Teacher Student Organization (PTSO) meeting in the evening. In between teaching from my living room and engaging with parents and the community online I ran outside to grab my headphones from my car. I immediately began to panic as I walked up to my little Jeep that had been ripped apart by a hit and run incident. Immediately after calling the police, I told my principal I would be a little late to the meeting. As a jack of all trades, he was very familiar with the automotive industry. He also knew I had been dying to trade my Jeep in for a Ford F-150, my dream car. As a fellow pickup truck enthusiast, he suggested I skip the PTSO meeting altogether, get out of the house, and go take a test drive or two. He explained that dealers were desperate to make a sale and it would be worth a shot. I thought about it and, knowing I would never be able to afford it, I took his advice anyway and went on a test drive. I signed the papers for my truck in November of 2020. Buying my dream car was always part two of the vision for me. I always thought, "grad school first, pickup truck second." This was where it clicked, and the lightbulb finally came on. If buying my dream car and working from home or school—depending on our outbreak status that week—was easy ... then what else was easy? That's when I first thought about grad school.

Fast forward a month or two later, teachers are finally allowed back in the building, and I am driving my shiny new truck to school only to walk upstairs to a room devoid of students, logging in and out of each class on a shortened schedule. I adapted to vastly different teaching environments once every few years, so switching up my teaching style was not a new concept for me. I knew what I could and could not accomplish teaching online and felt there was no unsolved problem I could fix. I was bored and just upset that my kids were not in front of me. I did not have enough time to get through full lessons online with the shortened schedule, so I worked with what I had, fully knowing my students were suffering academically. I felt helpless. While society painted a picture of online school as this incredible and amazing thing teachers did, I felt that no matter what I did during online learning, it would never be enough. Many people who had little to no experience with computers used their passion for education to fuel their ability to learn. But I did not need to learn. I was born into the world of technology, and it had been a passion of mine my whole life. I did not feel that I was doing anything amazing. I felt stuck and I knew I was not utilizing my professional capacity to its fullest potential. I just did not know what that looked like for me.

Once word got out about some things I was doing online with my students, I finally started to figure out what I had to offer. My colleagues, knowing I was completely obsessed with educational technology (and just technology in general), started coming to me for help. I had teachers from all over the district, across different grade levels and disciplines, coming to *me* for advice. Who was I to tell them how to teach? I was only a third-year teacher! But, somehow, my passion for education and my passion for technology came together and I made an impact for students outside of my own classroom. I was not just helping students, but I was helping adults too. Now, for the second time, I felt responsible for my school.

I reflected on the satisfaction I felt from the FireTide chats and helping my colleagues with educational technology and immediately fell in love with the idea of making an impact on students outside of my classroom. I will never forget when I first asked my principal about furthering my education. We talked about some options, and he told me to go do my research and get back to him. I went online and started researching graduate programs in education. That is when I saw the 14-month, fast track program in educational leadership, most of which was being done online due to the pandemic. That was it. That was the one. I came back the next day and we sat down to have a meeting about my future. The rest, as they say, is history. I became an educational leader because of COVID-19. I became an educational leader because it was easy.

I know I would not have started graduate school this early if it were not for the pandemic. I also believe I would not have gone for educational leadership right away if I was not forced to solve problems in education that required a computer. Yet here I am, graduating in three months, with a 4.0 grade point average. I even passed the state test, the School Leaders Licensure Assessment (SLLA), with flying colors, which I took at home on my laptop. I do not even have enough years of teaching experience to receive my certificates by graduation. I will simply apply to the state on my own once I have the required years of experience, rather than the school doing it on my behalf. Now, that is not to say I would not feel confident to become a principal right away. As I mentioned before, computers are where I thrive. I was able to learn on my own by navigating self-directed online lessons. I did just as much work as a student attending an in-person program, I just did it on my own time. If you asked me before I started graduate school if I preferred this over in-person learning, I would have absolutely, without a doubt, said no. I hated online learning. During my undergraduate work I would never take the online option, were it available. But the pandemic changed my mind. I no longer prefer in-person learning because it is not as easy for me. With online learning, I do not have to get in the car and drive to class. I do not have to pay for gas, food, and parking. I would never be able to do all that as a fourth-year teacher. I would not be able to afford it. I could not give up my coaching position and the extra jobs I get paid for at school. I would lose my apartment. Now, I can work all those extra hours and still complete all my work on time. For me, it was easy.

The only difficult part of the program for me was definitely the internship. Not because of the difficulty of the work, but, obviously, because of the hours. Those hours could not be done at 3 o'clock in the morning once I finished working, doing additional school-related jobs for extra money, finding time to eat dinner, and picking up cat food from the pet store. Although it was certainly difficult to complete my 300 internship hours, every minute was worth it. Anything I may have missed out on by not attending in-person classes, I made up for by learning from my principal during this time. Much like myself, he became an educational leader at a young age. By being fearless, intelligent, and unbreakable, he quickly became successful in education, his second career. Moving from teacher to supervisor, then from assistant principal to principal, he was running a high school in his early 30s.

When I asked my principal if he would mentor me for the duration of my internship, I was delighted that he accepted. I watched his leadership closely and began to model my practice after his. I knew what I should and should not do from the countless online textbooks I read for my coursework, but I needed to learn how to *act* like a leader. I will never forget the last faculty meeting we had before we went out for the rest of the school year when the pandemic first hit. He was under extreme pressure and still remained cool, calm, and collected. People were asking him questions that he could not answer because there was no answer. But he did not get frustrated. He did not raise his voice. He calmly acknowledged everyone's feelings, agreeing with the severity and uncertainty of the situation. He then shared his own feelings and related to everyone in the room, bringing levity to the situation when he said, "you can't make this stuff up." He consistently maintained clear, transparent communication with his constituents throughout the entirety of the pandemic. Just this year, about two years after the aforementioned faculty meeting, we had another one right before we went on winter break. He told the staff that no one, himself included, knew if we were coming back into the building after the break. He still did not have all the answers but had a way of reassuring everyone in the room. I imagine my leadership will look something like that. Complete and total uncertainty with a touch of passion, care, and confidence. He faced an unforeseeable future but adapted to it with ease. And so will I. When you have no choice but to adapt to unforeseen circumstances, time and time again, when that is all you know, it becomes the one thing you can do best. Because it's easy.

CHAPTER 9

ON THE BRINK OF LEAVING

Abigaile Almerido

"You have high blood pressure."

I have always been teetering on the edge of hearing those exact words. I have a menu of underlying health conditions stemming from my family's history. My people's food pyramid embraces rice, sugar, and pork, and my father passed away two years and one month prior from complications of heart surgery. I am not surprised, but I am fearful.

That day, I began to take deeper stock of what was going on in my life. I bought a home blood pressure monitor, began documenting my daily average heart rate, recommitted to a work-out regimen, checking food labels for sodium and sugar, actually heeded my Apple Watch's prompts to breathe, and began looking for patterns in my behavior that could help me course correct. I was determined to map my way backwards to a healthy body.

Over time, my average blood pressure and daily heart rate showed a steady decline.

In all my efforts to restore my mind and body, there were so many variables I could control in my personal life and yet when I looked to shift what was happening in my professional life, there seemed to be very immovable parts. My meetings were set, the work had to get done, the e-mail had to be sent. I found so many rules about how to conduct myself in work; rules I saw cemented into the earth. Furthermore, I was filling up my entire waking day with work and acting in such a way that severely limited my body and mind's opportunity to relax and recover from work. I was eating lunch at my desk, constantly thinking about messages I needed to send, or actions I needed to take to move a project along while I was driving or brushing my teeth. I found myself idly checking e-mail after work in the same way I browsed my social media. What I found was that I could not separate healthy me outside of work and healthy me during work. I had to find a way to be healthy. Period.

This was the challenge. I will, at the time of this publication, have worked remotely for two years. Yes, this comes from a severe state of privilege. Yes, there have been folks who have not once had the joy and the pain of reconfiguring one's home and life to make even more space for work. Yes, most of the public education work is already back to working in-person. I am not even part of those masses; I am not a classroom teacher dealing with ever-changing health policies on how to keep dozens of humans that share the same space 6+ hours a day from contracting this very unpredictable, air-borne virus. I am not a classroom teacher dealing with the deluge of what I can and cannot teach in the classroom. I am not a classroom teacher faced with saving the economy, upholding democracy, and doing it all for the children all before the lunch bell. Yet I am still burnt out, and in a way that feels unique to the times we are experiencing now.

The details of this burn out seem so mundane—the timeline is hardly worth mentioning. Like so many, working from home created an exponential increase in the number of meetings I was required to attend, and as a result increased my time spent on screen. After that, it was simple arithmetic … 4-5 hours of Zoom meetings + work created during meetings = continuous eyestrain + irregular headaches – time to do the actual work – time to connect with others in meaningful ways, minus, minus, minus.

Therein lies the extractive and subtractive nature of our field. As the challenges increase (and they continue to increase and become more prevalent as we grapple with teaching and learning during global crises), the demands of our roles expand, and the toll becomes unforgiving and certainly unrewarding. The work felt boundless, while the return to the individual felt limited and diminished. I found myself strapped with a dilemma I just could not reconcile: How could an institution that claims to be so people-oriented also be so little about the care for the people within it?

It's Time to Give Up Work-Life Balance

Did work cause my diminished health? For certain, work is not the only culprit. I take responsibility for choosing fries over broccoli, TV binging over jumping jacks, and Words with Friends over sleep. I have also chosen e-mail over rest, spreadsheets over leisure, Zoom meetings over recovery. What became glaringly evident throughout this pandemic was that, for all the choices that I made throughout the day, work would never choose me. Sure, work chose me for additional assignments to aid in the pandemic response, for extra meetings, for extra committees. To be sure, these choices are indications that my work and opinions are valued. I relish the feeling that I contribute to our organization in positive ways. And yet, for the all the ways work chose me, I have come to expect that it would never choose my physical health and my mental wellness over its own products and outcomes. This does not mean there are not people at my work who care about me. On the contrary, I work with compassionate and loving individuals who show up for me in ways I would not typically expect of a coworker. The people are not the problem. The culture and the climate are. So, I have chosen me.

Choosing me was not easy and it did not come without tension or guilt. There is a running internal dialogue of me feeling mischievously selfish when I take a full lunch hour and after the 10 minutes I spend in the act of eating, I sit and watch an entire episode of a TV series I have already seen multiple times over. Choosing me has meant eating my lunch away from a monitor. It has meant me taking walks, sometimes twice a day. It has meant shutting my laptop down right at 5:00 P.M. and declining meeting invitations before 8:00 A.M., after 5:00 P.M., and especially at 12:00 P.M.—choosing me started out very clinically. It has meant taking "just one more e-mail" and "All I have to do is this one little thing before ..." out of my conversational repertoire. It has meant turning down last-minute projects when I know I have not been given enough time to prepare. I'm not batting a thousand in all these commitments, and I still feel that part of me is not doing the right thing by not filling every moment with work and pressure. Saying "no" to others is always a challenging commitment to hold to. It inevitably results in someone not getting the support they are seeking, and to me that seems counter to the educator's call. This makes me feel even more that somehow, I am not holding up my end of the bargain. But then I remember the meetings I took at lunch time, or the evenings I spent finishing presentation slides, or the way I changed plans with friends or family to accommodate more work getting done. It is then when I remember I have the receipts to show I have proven my worth and then some.

Saying "yes" to me and "no" to work has required regular self-reflection and presently involves a lot of bargaining. I have, at times, found myself disappointed with my choices; I question if my choices equate to failure on my part; failure to meet my career goals; failure to live up to some unspoken educator code that says: "We will give all of ourselves for the children." It has also taken many reminders from friends and colleagues to convince me that I was not choosing myself over equity work. They remind me that my heart has not left students, not left my internal drive to change conditions for those most injured by our systems. Rather, my heart has left existing in spaces where more energy is put into recruitment rather than retainment, where equity work is an outward endeavor and rarely an inward or multilateral one, where everything is an urgent matter except for taking care of oneself (and making sure our practices are not barriers to that), where "no" is a four-letter word. For someone whose role is to support workforce development and improve organizational culture, this is a hard pill to swallow.

What started as an exhaustion of my body grew into an exhaustion of my heart. My work's data was telling me I was not alone in my fatigue. One of my favorite parts of my current role is providing leadership coaching to my colleagues. Every time I meet with someone, for one full hour I am immersed in simply being helpful to someone else. That is my entire agenda. There is never an expectation in that hour that I stretch myself out to my capacity, never extra work generated, never pressure to fill every moment with something productive. Working through issues others are having feels so precious. Not only do I see my impact immediately, I am privy to individual experiences and emotions existing within our system. I hear so many stories. On a regular basis I have conversations with colleagues about navigating problematic behaviors from colleagues and supervisors—we build so many moats around people whose positional power makes open communication very difficult. Those I coach casually share they have regularly scheduled meetings during times that don't seem very conducive to excellent collaboration—who is truly at their best at 4 p.m. on a Friday afternoon? They are dealing with micro aggressions, macro aggressions, self-doubt, ever expanding work responsibilities, feelings of disengagement with their work all on top of whatever ails them in their personal lives.

This tumultuous sea of feelings is vast, complex, and nuanced. A colleague recently relayed to me this persistent feeling of "survivor's guilt." She shared this guilty feeling of starting a role that allowed her to have the space and time to think through the programs she managed, to really work within a 40-hour work week, to not have to push to her capacity's limits while she worked. Why is this not our baseline of expectation for our work? When did a 40-hour work week turn into a luxury rather than the norm? We have come to expect that our life's work will truly absorb our whole life that any time it is not infringing upon the other parts of our existence, there must be something wrong.

So, in addition to choosing me, I give up this notion of work-life balance. It is a myth and fundamentally backwards. The term came to popularity in the 1970s by Baby Boomers, primarily women who were trying to keep up with demands of employment, while raising families. The term has persisted in our vernacular simply because we exist in a culture that overvalues productivity at the expense of people. It places work first and life second.

It urges us to continue prioritizing what customarily should only represent 40 hours of a week and reinforces the belief that work is the primary function of life. So, I give up on work-life balance and choose life-work balance.

Self-Care is the Work of the Community

Part of my current role now is also to work with school and central office leaders to foster a climate of trust and belonging. Regularly, colleagues come to me or someone on my team describing what unfortunately has become very common: My staff is completely burnt out, followed by the equally common request: Can you work with them on learning self-care skills. Of course, there is a place for mindfulness in the classroom, and yes developing meditative and breathing practices and helping our colleagues tend to their mental and physical wellness has definite benefits. We certainly want our colleagues to place their proverbial masks on first. No question. Uplifting self-care and stress management strategies as the solutions to educator burn-out is, however, very limiting, and ultimately ineffective. When we place the responsibility on the individual to right the wrong, we absolve the system of its responsibility to care for the individual. Better breathing is only a band-aid. Our team members cannot meditate their way out of the working conditions that are producing their anxiety and stress.

What can be done then? At the 2021 Othering & Belonging Conference, the institute's director john a. powell spoke of the need for systems to return to infrastructures of care. To complement our insistence that individuals do what they need to take care of themselves, we also need to look at the ways in which our work culture supports our community in doing so. How do we envelope this ethos around an infrastructure of care in how we make decisions, how we relate and work with each other, and how we continue to take steps toward truly sustainable equity and belonging work?

What would it mean to really build and live within an infrastructure of care? Real care. Not just donuts. Our team members need true work reform to feel cared for, to expand the mental and emotional space they must continue to grow and collaborate within our field. As Rita Pierson, in her viral TEDTalk, proclaims, "Every kid needs a champion." Well, prospective and current school leaders, every educator needs a champion, too. Here is what leaders can do to begin to prioritize rest and make care of individuals a systemic policy:

Normalize working within—not beyond—the workday. This may take some serious reconditioning. Somewhere along the line, being a public educator in America meant cosigning a culture where working beyond our means was a badge of honor, sometimes even a measure that we were doing our work well. I have met countless educators who are so giving of their hearts and of their time for their students and their work. Their life's blood, sweat, and tears are so intricately tied to their identity as teacher, as caretaker, and as helper that the stance of giving is so natural. What happens when this is coupled with a working institution, which has a natural state of taking? If we are to retain those who continue to persist in our field, we must take honest assessment of what we ask of those in our care. Further, we must look at how our behavior, our language, our policies, and our intentions communicate what kind of life-work balance we value. We cannot treat our team member's good will to say yes as an endless resource. To truly normalize working within a workday, we must interrogate the cultural practices that got us so far off track. Here are some to consider (see Table 9.1).

Table 9.1

How Leaders Normalize Work Behaviors

Ways we normalize…	
Working beyond the workday	Working within the workday
Congratulating someone for always being the first to work and the last to leave	Setting boundaries around when work starts and stops (for yourself and for others)
Responding to and writing e-mail after hours (and even on weekends)	Saving the e-mail for tomorrow (or, if you must, scheduling the e-mail to be sent tomorrow) AND keeping your work e-mail app off your phone
Eating lunch and working.	Eating lunch.
Creating agendas that fill every minute and have huge potential for generating hours of work outside the meeting	Facilitate meetings that incorporate higher collaboration-to-information giving ratios.
Canceling or shortening vacation days to complete more work.	Putting your work out of your mind when on vacation.
Scheduling/Accepting meetings before or after work hours. Scheduling/Accepting meetings during lunch hours.	Just saying no.

Will we never engage in behaviors in the left column? Not likely. Our challenge is tipping the scale, so we are making working within the workday the norm and working beyond the workday more irregular.

Give your people a break. Yes, a literal break. Cancel the meeting, tell them to go home early, and if you're a district leader, this may even look like replacing in-service days with full rest days. In October 2021, the Alhambra Unified School District board and executive cabinet canceled professional development activities set for a student-free workday to provide staff a day to "use for any revitalizing activity that feels right to you." In November 2021 the Hazelwood School District extended their Thanksgiving break for students and educators, citing that the mental well-being resource they all needed was "time to rest and renew." As leaders at every level of the organization, how are we building intentional rest into our work? Exhaust does not produce the best work or most creative solutions, nor does it nurture the healthiest and strongest relationships.

Do more with more (or Do less with more). With limited budgets, we in education have always conditioned ourselves to leverage our resources, make do with what we have, stretch our pennies, and find creative ways to use our time and our personnel. This is certainly not new to our profession. What is new are all the unforeseen demands the pandemic put on our workforce that resulted in very short learning curves and adapting to ever-changing policies, structures, and conditions. What educators accomplished at the end of the 2020 school year to rapidly transition to distance learning was nothing short of miraculous. Communities came together to ensure families had increased internet and computing device access. Teachers, with varying degrees of comfort and competency in integrating technology put aside their fears to make sure students had increased access to their classrooms. Now that we have returned to in-person instruction, educators have even more roles to fill. They are nurses and social workers. They are mask monitors and physical distance officers. They are in-person, virtual, hybrid, and independent study facilitators of learning. And they have no more left to give. Our staffs cannot growth mindset or breathe their way out of limited hours and limited energy in a day. So, consider this paradigm shift. How do we do more with more support, more resources, more time? If no additional support, resources, and time are available, how do we make do with the results and work we currently have?

Say and hear the word "no" better. Sometimes prioritizing the rest and care of your people means being able to set boundaries in conversations your staff are not a part of (and then work toward making it so your staff is represented in these conversations in meaningful ways). This might mean saying no to that "one more thing" about to be added to your staff's plate. It might mean delaying a project until there are adequate resources to support the project. And it certainly means listening in to when team members say no, with their words or their actions.

Foster a working climate where saying "no" is not scary, but appreciated. In the Othering & Belonging Conference mentioned above, Alok Menon said, "Boundaries are how I love you and myself at the same time." Particularly in a time when the people within our systems are taxed to their capacity, we want to make sure our teams know they can and should communicate boundaries. For many educators, this will take more reconditioning. We are the people who help and often find it hard to be the people who also need help. Offering the opportunity to voice concerns and say no is not likely enough. Leaders in our field must also examine the cultures they've created and really interrogate if the culture fosters psychological safety. According to Tim Clark (2020), there are four stages of psychological safety:

- Inclusion Safety: Do I belong?
- Learner Safety: Am I growing?
- Contributor Safety: Can I make a difference?
- Challenger Safety: Can I question and challenge the status quo?

If your team members are not apt to share their opinions and concerns, it is time to invest in understanding why and finding some fixes.

Just ask. You work with brilliant minds and should make a practice of engaging in empathy exercises when designing for others. Consider how you could enlist your staff as partners in this effort to make more time and space for care. Empathy exercises could include surveys, ethnographic interviews, and focus groups. You could make the primary focus of one-on-one meetings you have with your team members conversations on care and support. Do any of these so long as you are listening and seeing results in response and change.

Walk a day in their shoes (on a regular basis). Fortunately, and unfortunately, school leaders across the nation have had to fill the shoes of teachers in response to a severe shortage of substitute personnel. Superintendent Georgeanne Warnock's TikTok account "The Subbing Superintendent" went viral in late 2021 for her posts on the experiences she had substituting in classrooms that had no coverage. Having this direct insight into some of the woes her staff is experiencing while teaching during the pandemic has provided this superintendent clear data that can inform how to adjust the practices in her district to make learning and teaching a little more hospitable. Many of her posts address the plummeting staff morale she is witnessing firsthand. Some of her more popular posts discuss ways she and her district leaders can meaningfully take things off the plate of teachers and administrators. How might school and central office leaders take this opportunity to be reflective of the practices and policies that impact the lives of their teams? In what ways are leaders accurately understanding what is on their team members' plates and in what ways are leaders actively looking to make that load lighter? The best way to help team members mitigate high levels of anxiety and stress will always be to work to remove the conditions that encourage these toxic aspects of a school leaders day.

And also, don't stop buying the donuts.

What Happens If We Don't

For the last week or so, Beyonce's song "Irreplaceable" (2006) has been running in my head (and sometimes sung out loud) as a soundtrack to my writing. She sings of a relationship past its prime, its joy, its usefulness, its vibrancy. Well, public education institutions, I am singing this song to you too. Gone are the days when educators inhabited the same classroom, teaching the same grade level for 30 years. With our current attrition rate, it is lucky if we keep folks on the books for more than five years. What makes our industry feel the conditions our team members are working in will keep them coming back for more?

We are running our people ragged and expect them to come back every single day. Our people are not ok. We are dying in a field that should be all about life giving. When we do not change the way we work and relate to uphold the status quo, we tell our people they are dispensable and that we are a simple recruitment away from filling their shoes. What a costly mistake is. Every time an educator walks away from a district, they take with them the learning that district paid for in conferences and workshops. They walk away with institutional knowledge of systems and of communities. They leave immeasurable impact in their absence.

Educators have amassed highly valuable skills, before and because of the pandemic. They are Google suite wizards. They can facilitate learning in a multitude of modalities. They are experts at engaging audiences. They are task masters, program managers, family influencers, and event planners. They are scholars of human motivation, content creators, artists, and makers. Former educators I know have gone onto successful careers in curriculum design, family photography, and leadership development. Private sector companies, educational and otherwise, have teams ready to welcome our very highly skilled workforce. Where will they go to? Wherever they please.

REFERENCES

Beyonce. (2015). Irreplaceable [Song]. On *B'Day*. Sony Music.
Clark, T. R. (2020). *4 stages of psychological safety: Defining the path to inclusion and innovation*. Berrett-Koehler.

CHAPTER 10

FROM TEACHER TO EDUCATIONAL LEADER

Reflections Upon Educator Identity in the Midst of the COVID-19 Global Pandemic

Maria Leyson

INTRODUCTION

More than ever before in the recent history of this nation, educators are compelled to confront the biases that have shaped teaching practices in our society and to create new ways of knowing, different strategies for the sharing of knowledge.

—hooks (1994, p. 12)

The words of bell hooks, from her 1994 book, *Teaching to Transgress*, illuminate our experiences today as educators and educational leaders. Here, she explores race and race relations in the face of racial oppression in the public education system. Her words still ring true more than 30 years after the initial publication of this book, in the face of a global pandemic that has forced us to face the racial, economic, and social disparities that have been festering within the American public education system.

Admittedly, I did not notice this festering in my work as a classroom teacher right away. Nor did I start to understand my own identity as an educator for years, until my third year as a classroom teacher when a sudden influx of students from my district's Special Education preschool were assigned to my General Education kindergarten class. While I had had a bit of experience of working with students with Special Needs and students who are classified as English Learners, I finally saw the extent to which I was not prepared. In that school year, I started to truly see greater systemic disparities in which I was working.

The families in my class, many of whom were BIPOC (Black, Indigenous, and people of color) and of immigrant-origins, shared their stories of navigating the Special Education system: their confusion about the English Learner classification, what it meant to have a children with Special Needs and the effects of this label upon their futures, and how to even begin to navigate a school system that was so foreign to them. I saw myself in the community in which I was teaching, having grown up a child of Filipino immigrants, raised in a neighborhood surrounded by peers with similar backgrounds: BIPOC, first generation, immigrant, blue collar. I identified closely with my teachers and counselors, many of whom were immigrant families themselves. Years later, I was drawn to work in schools with similar make-up to those I attended. As an Asian American educator herself, Yoon (2019) states:

> Reflecting on my teaching experience as a female teacher of color created inner tensions and emotional struggles to a great degree. Nonetheless, it also allowed me to positively rethink my own position and roles as a critical educator. (p. 92)

I saw so much of myself in the students and the families in my school community. The intersections of my personal being began to merge with my professional identity with the acknowledgment I was not only a teacher, but a female, Asian American educator. In this particular school year, just a few years before the COVID-19 global pandemic, my identity as an advocate for marginalized communities, especially BIPOC students and families, started to bud.

I developed a growing awareness of the intersections of race and class when I started college at a large, public university in the San Francisco Bay Area in a metropolitan area close to my hometown. There, I had classmates whose backgrounds were so vastly different from mine, whose experiences, and privileges I had never experienced. There, I became acutely aware that I was one of the few Filipino Americans in any given space which I entered. Over time, I found mentors and friends on the campus, but spent a large part of my undergraduate life trying to find where I belonged, to find representations of myself. Even at a large, progressive university such as the one I attended, I continued to struggle to find a sense of belonging, to find reflections of myself in my surroundings, to find others whose origin stories matched my own.

In the following narrative, I will reflect upon my positionality as a classroom teacher, specifically, a female, Filipino American teacher at an urban elementary school in the San Francisco Bay Area in the midst of the COVID-19 global pandemic. In this reflection, I will explore spaces of transition and flux as I evolve in identity from classroom teacher to educational leader to educational researcher. I will reflect upon my critical awareness of race, disability, and socioeconomic status as I, in the words of bell hooks (1994), attempt to transgress systems of oppression, and find joy in teaching and learning, again.

Global Pandemic

It was an unforgettable Friday the 13th, the last "normal" day of instruction before the effects of COVID-19 took hold of the schools and communities in the nine counties of the San Francisco Bay Area in which I live and work. That afternoon I sat in my colleague's classroom, simply waiting. My colleagues and I were waiting for any direction, any news of what to do with this coronavirus outbreak that was sweeping all over the world. We heard that schools around us were shutting down, some for deep cleaning of classrooms until this mystery disease passed. Many districts were going to shut down for just a couple weeks, just up to Spring Break, and my colleagues and I anticipated the same thing.

While waiting for directions about this mysterious virus, I was also awaiting a call from the assistant superintendent of human resources (HR) about a disturbing incident concerning the principal at my site. I was one of two site union representatives that school year and tensions were high between the staff and this principal. My union counterpart and I found ourselves in the middle, shuffling messages between the leadership and the teachers, between the principal and her staff, and we were finally at the breaking point where district leadership was now involved. I was in the throes of an administrative credential program where the central philosophy was to hold the mindset of an educational leader, not simply part of "middle management," "administrator." In this small leadership role as a union representative in conjunction with my studies, I saw firsthand the importance of relational trust and communication.

On this day, on the eve of the shelter-in-place orders around the Bay Area, I was immersed in a space that was heavy with the need for healing: a new principal looking to assert herself, teachers and staff seeking to be seen and heard. There were so many issues that had been brought up in the months leading up to the pandemic, all seeming to burst at the seams:

student discipline, school climate, building and facilities, instructional leadership. So many needs needed to be addressed. I sat in on numerous school leadership meetings in which teachers voiced the great social, emotional, and academic concerns for their students. In turn, they were offered professional development opportunities and boxes of books and curriculum to fill the gaps, simple band-aids to greater systemic issues, they would express later.

In a sense, the conversations between the teachers, staff, and leadership in the time leading up to the pandemic were not much different than they are now, in the middle of the omicron surge at this moment of this writing. Our already fragile system was at its breaking point at the cusp of the pandemic and broke as we launched headfirst into shelter-in-place.

After hanging up the phone with the assistant superintendent of HR, my colleagues and I received the news we had anticipated: two weeks of school shutdowns to allow for deep cleaning, with an extended shut down into Spring Break, if needed. That was it. We were to send work for students to work on at home and keep ourselves on stand-by for the next steps.

We teachers were instructed to give students and families a few days to reestablish themselves as offices, factories, and industries as the entire Bay Area all shut down to go into "distance learning," a term none of us had ever heard before. My colleagues and I stuffed envelopes full of worksheets and homework packets, enough to last the students for at least the next two weeks. Many of the students and families were able to pick up their materials and technology such as Chromebooks; but just as many did not. Despite being situated near the heart of Silicon Valley and surrounded by the headquarters of tech giants such as Google and Facebook, we learned that many families in our school community did not have access to reliable devices or the internet. I was surprised to learn just how many families did not have the very tools needed to connect with us, the teachers, and the world beyond our students' homes. While I was vaguely aware of this disparity, it became glaring to me as we transitioned into distance learning.

The first two weeks were spent trying to get students and families the tools they needed to do schoolwork at home. When it was finally determined that we teachers would attempt to meet with our students using video conferencing platforms, I found myself in the mindspace of a novice teacher again, blind to the pedagogy and methods needed to teach effectively; I was in pure survival mode. The first virtual meeting with my kindergarteners was surprisingly joyful. Those who were able to login did so. They were excited to see each other and me over the screen, gleefully waving to each other and playing with the microphone on/off features. I spent that first session simply having the students share how they were doing. In the true nature of the early childhood classroom, my young students shared how happy they were to see me and each other. However, their parents and caregivers seemed resigned. I would later learn, they were being confronted with issues of race, economics, and health right off the bat, so early in the pandemic.

Most of my students came from immigrant, working class families, just like mine. I was immersed in the growing awareness of my role not just as a teacher, but an Asian American teacher. My primary role in this pandemic would be to maintain the relationship between the families and our school system. According to Kohli (2018),

> Research has demonstrated that teachers of Color play a vital role in remedying racial disparities of achievement (Villegas & Jordan Irvine, 2010), due in part to their commitments and passions to teaching within urban schools (Achinstein & Ogawa, 2011).... In addition, teachers of Color often have insight to the racialized experiences of students of Color and can support their effective navigation of structural barriers (Gomez & Rodriguez, 2011; Kohli, 2009; Mabokela & Madsen, 2007). (p. 5)

As a kindergarten teacher for the past six school years at the start of the pandemic, I had developed the philosophy that the role of the kindergarten teacher was to welcome students and families to our school community and to introduce them to the school system as a whole. But when I entered the world of distance learning, I felt the urgency in maintaining this relationship, even more so in truly seeing how the BIPOC and socioeconomically disadvantaged families in my class struggled to survive. The only way I knew how to build relationships over the screen was by keeping open lines of communication: daily emails, online and over-the-phone conferences, simply to check in on their physical and mental health. In these conferences with parents, I learned about the loss of jobs, racially motivated attacks on one of the Asian American families in my class, the health crises as a result of the virus. The relationships I developed with my students and their families deepened in our shared acknowledgement as people of color navigating systemic barriers both within the educational system and in the world around us, as we retreated further into the home for both physical and psychological safety.

In the early months of the pandemic, I became closer to the families in this class more than I ever had in my entire teaching career. While we were physically apart, there was closeness that was fostered as I conferenced with families individually and continued to meet with their children as a whole class. Through video conference, I was in their living rooms, on their kitchen counters, and as the weather transitioned from winter to spring, I joined the families in their backyards. I worried about the families who did not have access to technology, so we bridged the divide over the phone. My students' parents told me stories of their fears of the virus, of their fears of economic uncertainty. The Bay Area has the largest concentration of millionaires in the world, with high housing and living costs to go along with this. Many of the parents worked blue collar factory jobs. And many of those parents lost their jobs or became underemployed in the pandemic. The economic insecurity was overshadowed by the sheer terror of watching close family members fall ill to this unknown virus.

Conversations around race and racism came up in class session as one student of Chinese descent described a verbal attack upon his family. His mother and I talked after class, both of our identities as Asian American women at the forefront as we discussed the uptick of attacks against the Asian American community. This conversation continued schoolwide a year later as the attacks persisted primarily against Asian American elders in the Bay Area, a very real fear of mine as I worried about the physical safety of my own parents. My identity as a Filipino American woman started to really shape my identity as an educational leader as I saw the parallel between my experiences and those of my students and their families. Yoon (2019) references Hune (2011), in the particular experiences of Asian American women through the argument that our "experiences are distinctively shaped through the interlocking multiple hierarchies of gender, race, immigrant/citizen status, nationality, and language" (p. 82). The open conversations in my classroom community about these hierarchies that shaped our experiences in school and in society, brought us together. Relational trust was needed to cradle our physical and social vulnerabilities. I started to learn that educational leadership was not about "saving" the community, but in simply listening. Listening opens the door to true leadership by fostering that relational trust.

EDUCATIONAL LEADERSHIP

I started in the Preliminary Administrative Credential Program at a local university in my hometown in the fall of 2019, right before the beginning of the pandemic. I will never forget the very first reading assignment for this program: Gloria Ladson-Billings's (2006) work, *From the Achievement Gap to the Education Debt*. The sociopolitical, economic, historic, and moral debts to BIPOC students and community members stuck with me as a BIPOC teacher. I learned throughout the course of the administrative program that my experience in public education, both as a student and as a teacher of color, was by design. The disparities I had experienced, that I witnessed my students and their families experiencing, was by design. We were up against the machine of White supremacy and neoliberalism, immersed in an educational system and a society never built for people of color (Ladson-Billings, 2006).

I graduated from the administrative credential program in June of 2020. From home, I learned to analyze school resources, human and fiscal, for social justice, to use them to maximize advocacy for populations like our English Learners and students with Special Needs, the very population of students who were so critical in the formation of my identity as a classroom teacher. Three months into the pandemic, I was physically exhausted from the endless hours on the computer for both my work and coursework, but, spiritually and academically, felt freer than I ever had before. For the first time since my first year of teaching, I wanted to learn more. I wanted to know why the academic disparities I had witnessed my entire career never seemed to resolve themselves despite all of the reforms put into place, such as the purchase of new programs and new curriculum. I wanted to know why my site had experienced a revolving door of principals in the last five years, not a single one lasting more than two school years. I wanted to know how to create better working conditions for myself and my colleagues and better learning conditions for our students and families. I wanted to know why my daily existence, and that of my colleagues, had felt so heavy, despite small moments of joy with our students. I wanted to understand the weight I was carrying as a BIPOC educator teaching primarily BIPOC students.

Ladson-Billings's (2006) work laid the foundation to my wonderings: the continued and systemic invisibilization of BIPOC communities. I spent the summer of 2020 in professional development and community of practice meetings, planning for the upcoming school year. Meanwhile, the death of George Floyd and the Black Lives Matter movement was at the forefront of media in the Bay Area, as were the attacks upon the Asian American community. That fall, I returned to the classroom, I was reassigned to teach remotely in my district's virtual academy. While the shelter-in-place orders were still in place, I freed my mind by revisiting readings from the administrative credential program: Bettina Love's (2019) text on abolitionist teaching, *We Want to Do More Than Survive*, Paulo Freire's (1968) *Pedagogy of the Oppressed*, Gloria Ladson-Billings (2006) seminal work on the educational debt. Even in my favorite works of fiction, such as *Harry Potter*, I learned were commentaries on the educational system, race, and politics. I found solace in reading with the lack of safe physical space in which to engage in activism and conversation about race, economics, and politics.

I found solace in reading the words of fellow educators who wrote decades ago of the very disparities that were exploding right in front of me. In the virtual academy, I was assigned to serve students from two very different schools in my district: my home school and an affluent neighboring, non-Title I school. Over video conferencing, I could see the vast differences in my students' living conditions, a sight that I could not unsee. So that winter, I decided to take a leap of faith to return to the university. It was hard to sit back and to sit in the suffering of the pandemic, to witness the disparities unfolding before my very eyes on the computer screen. I applied to the Doctor of Education (EdD) program in Educational Leadership, with a focus on Social Justice at a local university in my hometown.

I thus entered the EdD program with this burning question: How could our neighboring, non-Title I schools (one of which is only 0.8 miles from my home school), have resources not available to my students? I wondered how I went for almost a decade as a classroom teacher without ever truly seeing these disparities. What can I do about this? What can we, as a community of educators, do about this?

(RE)IMAGINE

In the face of this pandemic, I urge you to reimagine your role as an educator and educational leader. There are so few of us left. Enrollment in teacher education and administration wanes year after year. We carry the weight of our classrooms and school buildings: these spaces are microcosms of our world. By extension, we could think of ourselves as carrying the weight of the world. My experiences in the Bay Area, though unique to me, will sound familiar to you. Instead of carrying the weight alone, actively find a community within your school, within your district or county, to take the load off. Educational leadership cannot be done by one principal, one superintendent, or one teacher in isolation: it is this very individualistic, neoliberal thinking that has contributed to breakdowns in our system. Over video conferencing platforms, I found solace and healing with my classmates in the EdD program, fellow Bay Area educators also seeking respite from the pain.

I urge you to reimagine spaces of learning. Create classrooms and schools that are responsive to student needs: their physical safety, their emotional and psychological safety. I urge you to put aside the "learning loss" and "educational gaps," and think about what the students and families really need: reassurance, consistency, and love. In the same school year, my students and I watched the horror of the January 6 attacks and watched in awe on inauguration day as we witnessed Kamala Harris, a Bay Area native, and first African American and South Asian woman sworn in as Vice President of the United States. It is not possible to focus on academics when racial, social, political, and economic factors directly affect your students and their families.

I urge you to reimagine what is being taught and studied. Bring in the students' lives, honor their cultures, respect the Indigenous land upon which you stand. Bring in the teachers' lives, honor their cultures, and acknowledge their concerns of their physical and emotional safety. Put their stories at the forefront of their educational experiences. People long to be seen and to be heard. See them, listen to their stories. In the 2020–2021 school year, I learned about the violent death of an older sibling of one of my students, an African American male, and first-handedly saw the family's grief in the face of mainstream White supremacist messaging and national cases of police brutality. As an educational leader, see your students and their families for who they are and respond to what they need.

I urge you to take a humanistic approach, grounding yourself in the humanity of this field. We, as educators and educational leaders, are fostering human beings, not test scores or statistics. Create space for love and joy.

REFERENCES

hooks, b.. (1994). *Teaching to transgress: Education as the practice of freedom.* Routledge.

Ladson-Billings, G. (2006). From the achievement gap to the education debt: Understanding achievement in US schools. *Educational Researcher, 35*(7), 3–12.

Kohli, R. (2018). Behind school doors: The impact of hostile racial climates on urban teachers of color. *Urban Education, 53*(3), 307–333.

Yoon, I. (2019). Rising above pain: An autoethnographic study on teaching social justice as a female teacher of color. *Journal of Cultural Research in Art Education (Online), 36*(2), 78–102.

CHAPTER 11

CAN ANYONE BECOME AN ABOLITIONIST EDUCATOR?

April J. Mouton

A Poetic Abolitionist Prologue

yearning
for the opportunity to create
opportunity for change
opportunity to love
radically
and care for children
access and relevancy
still
the constructs of a system that was
not designed for opportunities to create and change
not designed to serve and love my students
not designed to care for
black
me
so, honor ancestral knowledge and
dismantle

—April J. Mouton (2022)

INTRODUCTION

Schools have desperately needed an update to truly engage and reach students of diverse backgrounds. According to Payne (2008), previous school reform projects such as Success for All, America's Choice, and the School Development Program have failed to integrate the "globalization, the outmigration of jobs from central cities, the resegregation of schools … and isolation of the worst urban neighborhoods" (p. 3). Moreover, perhaps the definition and original foundation of schooling needed a reboot. Despite a system founded on Jefferson's goal to separate a "few geniuses from the rubbish" (The Equity Collaborative, n.d., p. 1), those that the system was never designed to serve have pushed back to ensure that acquiring an education became linked to a human right rather than a luxury. From Indigenous Americans fighting back to maintain and pass down their culture to the next generation, from slaves rebelling and learning how to read despite the fear of death, to Mexican Americans and African Americans establishing escuelitas and freedom schools to supplant the lack of cultural identity, language, and awareness integration in schools that recounted historical narratives from a White dominant-saviorism perspective. The laboring and non-elite have always had the tools, desire, and knowledge to design a learning environment of high scholars, rigor, and communal love (Barragán Goetz, 2020; Moses & Cobb, 2001).

> Prior to the COVID-19 pandemic's impact on the school system, some schools were attempting to deviate from or push the current system by creating systems that increased opportunities for historically underrepresented students to access more rigorous courses. They were truly engaged in a shift from reforming schools to abolishing our current system via engaging in more student-centered instructional models and increasing student's voice through collaborative learning models. Some fear that if schooling deviates too much, kids might not acquire the right skill sets, the skill sets that are tied to capitalism, a dominant culture's definition of responsibility and success. One of my colleagues shared that schools taught him how to be really good at being a good worker. But his schooling never taught him how to dream, how to be creative, how to be an entrepreneur, how to push the current system so that he was in control of his learning outcomes. As the focus on returning to normal outweighs those invested in the opportunity to think and design differently, the inadequacies of high-stakes assessments, educators' low expectations on students navigating poverty, and insufficient resources to support students that learn differently are spotlighted. (Love, 2020)

So, can everyone become an abolitionist educator? Is it possible for those who have not suffered systemic racism to embody radical joy? Love (2019) defines radical joy as a concept that "originates in resistance … discovered in making a way of our no way" (p. 15). Radical joy perseveres beyond pain to create access for our most vulnerable scholars. Are educators willing to pause and be reflective of their practice and look within for answers? When attending equity training, the first type of work that you are asked to do is to look within. But there is fear. There is fear in acknowledging one's own privilege. It is difficult to look within and acknowledge areas of the racist policy that you perpetuated. It is difficult to look within and realize that you consciously decided to go with the flow instead of responding to racist thoughts. It is difficult to look within and realize that you rationalized why police need to be on school campuses. You rationalized why there are not a lot of students of color in your gifted and talented community. You rationalized why some students will never learn calculus in your building.

Researchers such as Love (2019), Moore (2018), hooks (1994), share that the heart of abolitionist work is love. "Love is animated through our connections, mutual understanding, and community" (Moore, 2018, p. 325). Muhammad (2020) pushes educators to see love as "always knowing that we belong ... critical love works to disrupt and dismantle oppression" (p. 167). So, while people are excited to read the works of Bettina Love (2019), David Stovall (2018), Dena Simmons (2019), and others—while they are excited to dive into hooks's (1994), *Teaching to Transgress*; are they excited to pause to do the work? Can they all become conduits of radical joy? Do they believe that love is necessary in our schools? Is there a fear of becoming radical because it might disrupt the system that some have become so successful in navigating?

This chapter serves as an invitation to dialogue around the questions of who can and should do the work of educational abolitionism in our current school system? Using a kitchen-table talk protocol as a communal process of engagement, the voices of 8 educators of diverse backgrounds (by ethnicity, age, geographical location, religious affiliation, sexuality, gender, and years of educational experience), yet united in their passion to disrupt our current educational system, gathered around three virtual kitchen-table talk settings to share their abolitionist journeys. This chapter also serves as a space to honor the voices of those currently in the work navigating crippling COVID constraints, alongside the continued public slay of Black and Brown folx at the hands of a system stated to serve and protect but rooted in capturing and silencing. Thus, these dynamic educators along with the author offer found poetry pieces as a way of synthesizing a response to the opening question; can anyone become an abolitionist educator?

Disruption Inside a Pandemic: Minimizing Harm

In a 2021 Dave Chappelle special, Chappelle refers to once enslaved, William Ellison, who after becoming free and learning how to work the land, became a ruthless slave owner himself. Chappelle notes that Ellison's rationale for his brutal treatment of his slaves was that he simply followed the current blueprint of how to be successful (Lathan, 2021). Abolitionists strive to diminish the amount of harm that they cause to others. In Chappelle's set, while he brings light to the dynamic power of critical pedagogy by providing an example of institutionalized capitalism and violence on us, he shares this piece in a set where he gains laughs, applause, and publicity by pushing out jokes that provide direct harm to those that intersect the trans and Black community (Israel, 2021). Chappelle, perhaps unknowingly, is using his platform to bring harm to the concept of Black love. Despite his often-radical comedic approaches that can serve as a abolitionist approach towards dismantling systemic racially harming spaces, Chappelle's desire to uplift one group cannot come at the price of harming another. It is important that we do not confuse abolitionist work based solely on historical knowledge.

Moore (2018) defines Black radical love as a daily practice of "protecting Black life and emptying ourselves of the death-dealing practices of misogyny; trans and queer antagonism; ableism ... and any other act of lovelessness that aids in the killing of Black people's spirits and bodies" (p. 326). All of this nestled during the pandemic when the call to go back to "normal" as quickly as possible is fueled by capitalism, and at the cost of the alarmingly high percentage of deaths of poor, marginalized people of color (Centers for Disease Control and Prevention [CDC], 2020). Thus, abolitionist educators are encouraged to disrupt the current blueprint of what is successful (changing concepts of success strictly connected to test scores, income, and material gains) by limiting harm on others instead of notoriety.

After the public execution of Elijah McClain, George Floyd, and Ahmaud Arbery educators felt the tension between the comfort of their White privilege cloak and their internal turmoil to not let their silence be viewed as compliance, acceptance, or affirmation to the White supremacist building block of America. In response, many educators went out in masses to purchase Muhammad's (2020) *Cultivating Genius*, Kendi's (2019) *How to Be an Antiracist*, Love's (2019) *We Want to Do More than Survive*, Oluo's (2019) *So You Want to Talk About Race*, Morris's (2016) *Pushout*, Hammond's (2014) *Culturally Relevant Teaching and the Brain*, and others. There was this unspoken hope, that somehow reading about Black pain and struggle, or companies updating their websites with a Black Lives Matter solidarity statement, would somehow shift our country's longstanding history of the negative connotation lenses that so many Americans wear when they see Blackness.

Sadly, since Floyd's public execution 266 Black Americans have died via police force in 2021, with Black people being three times more likely to be killed by police compared to White people (Mapping Police Violence, 2022). This disproportionate disparity also shows up in our schools where Black students continue to be suspended and expelled at alarming rates compared to their White peers (National Center for Education Statistics [NCES], 2019). Even more troubling, the suspension and disciplining of Black students during the pandemic continued. Oppressive disciplinary practices were manifested through school mandates requiring that students' cameras be turned on during virtual instruction. Based on my observations, these mandates impacted Black students disproportionately. Furthermore, the policing of marginalized folks of color on the streets is replicated in our school buildings. Our students, our teachers of color, are struggling to carry this pain while navigating the weight of a pandemic (Love, 2020; Morrison, 2020).

In Dr. Patricia Virella's (2021) reflection on confronting colorblind crippling systems as a site leader, she embodies the call to action as an abolitionist educator by realizing that this work must go beyond book analysis and talk, but rather into expecting all of her teachers to "do the work during the school year in order to support [their] students in a space that would treat them with the integrity they deserved ... so educators would see the brilliance of the students they served" (p. 39). This act of disrupting systems that continue to criminalize students of color, of calling to the table the necessary actions and focus, is abolitionist education in action (Bolding et al., 2022). There is a difference between education and schooling. Cornel West said, "public education is predicated on the notion that you're concerned about other people's kids just as much as your own kids" (Meier & Gasoi, 2017, p. 137). If schooling is the gateway for a majority of children to access high levels of education, then we cannot simply improve our schools with new reforms for today's children when the initial system was never designed to serve them. We must disrupt, abandon, and reimagine. We must create space for radical thoughts and equip ourselves with the necessary tools and confidence to leverage our street capital, invest in our collaborative capital, honor, or imaginative capital, engage in radical action, and use our internal beating drums, to truly abolish and recreate (Bolding et al., 2022).

Defining Abolitionism

United States abolitionism is entrenched in a narrative of valuing identity or humanizing those that opposed supremacist ideology (Dillard & Neal, 2020; Riley & Solic, 2021; Stovall, 2018); which has been highlighted through slavery emancipation, woman suffrage, Black feminist movement, the rise of freedom schools during the civil rights movement, the new Jim

Crow of mass incarceration, the current school to prison pipeline, and so forth. "As prison abolitionists understand prison as a corrosive, dreading place intended to dislodge people of color from social fabrics that affirm and protect their existence, 'school' in the traditional sense should be considered in a similar vein" (Stovall, 2018, p. 56). Abolitionist teaching invokes the history of abolitionism; changing the narrative from altruistic Whites to profoundly imaginative and African Americans equipped to lead their fight beyond equality to true liberation (Neal & Dunn, 2020). Rooted in challenging systems of policing and imprisonment, abolitionists seek to minimize harm by recognizing when they may engage in replicating systems of harm and by being a champion for reconstruction, redesigning, and reimagining by acknowledging and cultivating the brilliance of students of color (Love, 2019; Muhammad, 2020). These educators resist cosigning to a pedagogy of poverty (Haberman, 1991), and instead adopt a more radical and engaged pedagogy that insists on teaching "in a manner that respects and cares for the soul of our students" (hooks, 1994, p. 13). The pandemic has publicly exposed that our most marginalized communities have inequitable access to advanced technological resources, a disparity in quality first instruction supports, and a lack of systems that uplift student and community voices. As educators navigate the current and future impacts of the pandemic on our educational system, those with an abolitionist mindset must, "[radically] dream, [they] must demand, and act" (Love, 2020, para. 1). Abolitionist work may not be for everyone. This work requires "teachers who are willing to place their power, privilege, and positioning on the line to dismantle oppressive structures that murder the spirits of Black children" (Neal & Dunn, 2020, p. 70).

Shifting From Ally to Coconspirator

The trend of being an abolitionist educator is not new. It is a trend that has always existed because there has always been a level of oppression, a level of being unseen in our schools. Unfortunately, a crisis, such as Black lives continuing to die at the hands of a White culture, and finally being recorded, finally, being brought to light has pushed those who have stood on the sidelines, who have not had to be affected, whose White privilege has shielded them—some of those folks are starting to come out into the light. Some of them are choosing to just be allies. Some of them are choosing to grab the mic and make it their movement. But the real folks are choosing to be coconspirators. They are choosing to allow their privilege to be at stake in order to disrupt and challenge the current system in order to foster equality and more importantly equity. As the COVID crisis impacts our schools, and educators must find new ways to connect with families and connect with students, many are realizing that a standardized test at the end of the year will never sum up a student's progress. Relying solely on an end-of-the-year standardized test to measure growth does not provide an opportunity for a student to share what they do know, but only highlights if they haven't had access the publishers' expectation of demonstrating understanding to the standard. Abolitionist educators must reimagine multiple ways for students to demonstrate their knowledge.

Riley and Solic (2021) note that teacher programs can develop coconspirators by being intentional about the community spaces in which we develop their skillset, noting that "teacher educators [must] think about their work in ways that are fundamentally different from traditional concepts of teacher educators" (p. 162). Love (2019) challenges educators to shift their focus on students' grit to recentering their approach to education by "taking small and sometimes big risks in the fight for equal rights, liberties, and citizenship for the dark child, their families, and their communities … [shifting from] a teaching approach to a way of life … a way of taking action against injustice" (p. 89). Coconspirators shift from mutually beneficial allyship work to "work for the benefit of groups of which they are not a member" (Hoffman & Martin, 2020, p.11). Furthermore, Love (2019) outlines this more dangerous role as a space where coconspirators "question their privilege, decenter their voices, build meaningful relationships with folx working in the struggle, take risks, or be in solidarity with others" (p. 117).

Kitchen Table Talks: Abolitionism, COVID, and Black Life

As an educational consultant supporting over 20 districts in Texas and Louisiana, I have been privileged to partner alongside teachers, principals, and district leaders as an instructional coach navigating the ever-changing impact of the pandemic on the landscape of educating and loving our future leaders. For some educators, COVID has paralyzed their ability to be creative in designing schooling opportunities for children, and thus the desire to control and enhance spaces of equality over equity guided their decisions. For others, the collision of Black lives dying at the hands of policing, at the hands of insufficient healthcare, and via erasure by critical race theory attacks were all rooted in a historical lineage of anti-Blackness (Love, 2019; McKinney de Royston, 2020). These moments became a catalyst to lean in on their abolitionists' roots and amplify their voices in protest on the streets, at the ballot boxes, and in classrooms. To highlight these current and aspiring leaders' voices, I engaged in a convenience sampling (Creswell, 2016) with 13 educators around the country that I have either supported, engaged in their research, or learned from. Five of the

13 educators were not able to participate in both the kitchen table talks and the found poetry follow-up session due to a family death (1), lack of availability (2), and lack of responsiveness (2). The following eight aspiring leaders engaged in both components of the oral narrative sessions:

Asha: mid-30s, East African Gujarati, queer female, with over 10 years' experience as an educator, currently an educational consultant and an adjunct university educator.

Gloria: mid-30s, Hispanic, bilingual, female, Christian, from central Texas, educator for over 15 years, currently looking for work as a classroom teacher because the previous site would not honor her request for a virtual setting due to health conditions.

- James: mid-40s, Black, heterosexual, male, Christian, from south Texas, educator for over 15 years, currently a classroom teacher.
- Jessica: mid-40s, White, Jewish, female educator from California, with over 20 years as an educator, currently a classroom teacher and coordinator.
- Monique: early-30s, Afro-Latina female, from New York, with over 10 years as an educator, currently a doctoral student
- Pedro: early-40s, male, bilingual, Chicano, Christian, with over 15 years as an educator, formerly a principal, currently a classroom teacher in California
- Robin: early-60s, Black, gay female, Episcopalian, an educator from the Western United States, over 35 years as an educator, currently a curriculum content developer/
- Shakira: early-30s, Black female, 10 years' experience in education, currently a principal in Colorado.

Kitchen-Table Talks

The use of roundtable meetings, pláticas, and circles are communal opportunities to engage in discussions (Guajardo & Guajardo, 2013). The kitchen-table talk has historical connections to slave abolitionists and civil rights activists as a space to problem solve, stay current in political movements, and to engage in community-focused spaces (Bolding et al., 2022; Haddix et al., 2016). All of these spaces are rooted in a foundation of traditional oral narratives (Sharpless, 2007). Due to the political, educational, and inequitable impact of covid in communities of color, the kitchen-table discussion style was ideal to increase a more fluid group conversation compared to a traditionally structured interview protocol. In my facilitated kitchen-table talks, the follow protocols were utilized:

- Lean into the conversation when ready.
- Actively listen by building on others' ideas and challenge others with questions.
- Be vulnerable by always speaking your truth.
- Confidentiality within the kitchen-table discussion.
- Speak from a place of love.
- Acknowledge if your comments have harmed others and seek to make amends.
- Utilize ancestral creativity and ingenuity.

The kitchen-table discussions centered around the following questions: What does being an abolitionist educator mean to you? Can anyone be an abolitionist educator or coconspirator? How has the pandemic impacted the abolitionist education movement? What challenges do our current educators face in taking on the role of abolitionists? How does love show up in our classrooms?

Found Poetry Exercise

"Poetry is not only dream and vision; it is the skeleton architecture of our lives. It lays the foundations for a future of change, a bridge across our fears of what has never been before."

—Audre Lorde

In an effort to humanize the experience of abolitionist educators' teaching and leading during the current COVID-19 pandemic, participants engaged in a found poetry exercise using their transcribed narrative from the kitchen-table talks. Just as abolitionist educators seek to reimagine (Dillard & Neal, 2020; Love, 2019), found poetry is the "rearrangement of words, phrases ... and reframing" (Butler-Kisbe, 2010). This deviation from more narrative traditional data sets provides the opportunity to honor participants' authentic voice by elevating emotive experiences in an artistic form (Butler-Kisbe, 2002; Sjollema et al., 2012), as well as bring a deeper understanding or new perspective to a phenomenon (Eisner, 1997). A common theme throughout the kitchen-table talks, and within the media during the pandemic, is the lack of heard voices—those of our educators and healthcare workers on the front line of this viral warfare, as well as the children and parents trying to balance the desire to learn and commune together with the constant fear of becoming too ill to recover. Thus, the use of participant-centered found poetry creates the stage to use "the art of poetry to explore and explicate the lived experiences" (Patrick, 2016, p. 386) of the participants in hopes to uncover invisibilities of a vulnerable and often marginalized group of educators (Sjollema et al., 2012). Participants had the option of creating a free verse found poem or a Malaysian pantoum poem, which are known for repetitive lines that help to evoke emotions (Pithouse-Morgan, 2016). Below are eight poems, highlighting aspiring educational leaders' thoughts and ideas as they voice their experience navigating in our educational system as they maneuver through a pandemic and heightened attacks on erasing Black contributions through critical race debates, all while attempting to be a source of hope and love for their students.

"Surviving co-optation"

by Asha (2022)

Abolitionism.
You're not ready.
'Educator':
inherent tie between institution and capitalism.
That ain't it.
It's not what the kids want.
Another
Diversity, Equity, and Inclusion training.
We don't want you on our team to stay on the sidelines.
I don't trust 96% of it.
Glimmers of hope.
Glimmers of opportunity,
but until black and brown trans queer neurodivergent disabled educators are leaders,
I don't trust anybody.
Returned to ideology and pedagogy,
a place of solace in the
day to day
context to the greater
historical hegemony.
Hip hop gave me consciousness before I had one.
inception,
seed planted,
and fostered experience.
Not everybody can be an abolitionist educator.
I say that unequivocally.

The articles,
the books,
affirm what's already there.
The possibility of the classroom to
imagine radically
beyond limitations.
Believe within yourself.
Because you can see it.
You can feel it.

I'm Fighting for You

by Gloria (2022)

I've done the work
Disrupting culture
Despite the lack of support
Teachers do have power; they do have a voice.

Disrupting culture
Difficult employees
Teachers do have power; they do have a voice.
Difficult employees

Difficult employees
Despite the lack of support
Difficult employees
I've done the work

They push you out when you fight back
You continue to battle
It's exhausting
We entered with blinders

You continue to battle
Still, these young people share their gifts
We entered with blinders
Despite minimizing who they are.

Still, these young people share their gifts
It's exhausting
Despite minimizing who they are.

98   A. J. MOUTON

They push you out when you fight back

Encourage them to showcase their voices and talents
Be proud and be willing to stand for something.
Say something.
It's nothing new. It's the system, yet again.

Arde means burn.
Be proud and be willing to stand for something
It's nothing new. It's the system, yet again.
A flame inside me, ingrained in my spirit, in my soul, in everything I do

Be proud and be willing to stand for something
Say something.
A flame inside me, ingrained in my spirit, in my soul, in everything I do
Encourage them to showcase their voices and talents

I'm fighting for you.
I'm fighting for me.
I'm fighting for children.
I'm paving my own way.

I'm fighting for me.
Demanding better for teachers.
I'm paving my own way.
Demanding better for our kids.

Demanding better for teachers.
I'm fighting for children.
Demanding better for our kids.
I'm fighting for you.

Pedagogy of the Hunted

by James (2022)

I had to take a break. I'm sorry.
And I have a lot of mixed feelings about the whole situation, mixed between rage and
You cannot defeat a system with a program
I would say that being an abolitionist educator looks like challenging the status quo

And I have a lot of mixed feelings about the whole situation, mixed between rage and
I think we all learn from wherever we are, and then what we bring to the classroom.
I would say that being an abolitionist educator looks like challenging the status quo
The goal of education is to get you to say this is black or this is white, there's a God in heaven or there's not but it's your choice.

Because I think we all learn from wherever we are, and then what we bring to the classroom.
You cannot defeat a system with a program
The goal of education is to get you to say this is black or this is white, there's a God in heaven or there's not but it's your choice.
I had to take a break. I'm sorry.

You just need to get the shit out the way and let them do the best they can do–give them the information and if they decide to do nothing with it, that's on them

But you're not going to walk out of my space and say, Well, you know that big brother didn't teach me enough
I don't care what the system does to me any longer. I used to.
I might get fired or blackballed.

But you're not going to walk out of my space and say, Well, you know that big brother didn't teach me enough
How can you blackball somebody who already has black balls?
I might get fired or blackballed.
I guess in a way I'm hunting the system down because as long as I stay in it, they can't stop me.

How can you blackball somebody who already has black balls?
I don't care what the system does to me any longer. I used to.
I guess in a way I'm hunting the system down because as long as I stay in it, they can't stop me.
You just need to get the shit out the way and let them do the best they can do–give them the information and if they decide to do nothing with it, that's on them

Who is Valued?

by Jessica (2022)

To be a part of US public schools means

An obsession with ranking
With scores
With testing
With data

Ranking+Scores+Tests=Value

Who is valued?
Who is wanted?

These questions aren't openly discussed
The answers aren't pretty
They aren't democratic
They aren't just

But let's be honest
Some students are valued
Others aren't
Some families are valued
Others aren't
Some schools are valued
Others aren't

Where will you send your child?

Please look beyond
Rank
Tests
Scores

Look for passion
Look for courage
Look for dedication
Look for love

A Love Letter to Abolitionists Educators

by Monique (2022)

Dearest abolitionist educators,
uprooting existing systems and structures
omitting harm

a love ethic, starts internally
you get what you need
YOU gotta be well to do the work.
the grief and the pain, the mourning pushes– a vehicle
to joy

it's hard.it takes a toll.this neoliberal factory.
Let hope be your discipline (See Kaba)
youneedyoujustasmuchastheyneedyou
Rely on intergenerational love– the elders be knowin'
For the folks who blazed this path for us
Their history. Their work. Grounds.
Taking care of yourself, to fight
Is not merely a love ethic, but an act of resistance
You be well,
YOU gotta be
to do the work.

Mi granito de arena

by Pedro (2022)

We need to disrupt the system!
Communities have been minoritized, this cannot be ignored in schools
We must go head on against, policies, biased curriculum, inhumane pedagogical practices that are detrimental to the communities we love

We strive to bring in student voice
To validate their multiple languages and linguistic wealth
To celebrate their linguistic capital, familial capital, social capital, etc.
Our message is, "you're valuable and what you have to say is valuable"
Students respond, "my language matters. I have value, I have wealth."
This form of pedagogy is foreign to them though it shouldn't
They should feel and know that they are valuable
That they can make a difference
That they can resist
That they can dream.

But can we also survive and thrive in the institution of Education?
Are their allies like true allyship?
How do we sustain each other in this work within a biased and racist institution?

If I really want to resist, I need to transform myself within the system and fight back

Are you part of the problem? Or are you part of the real solution?

And if you are a part of the solution, then you must stay committed to challenge dominant practices. Transformative resistance!

You must bring in your whole self and be willing to reflect and learn with one another

Ally or Abolitionist?
When the hell are you going to do something?

by Robin (2022)

Is it education for liberation or liberation education?
Caught up now in semantics, a distraction from the work.
Everyone wants to do the book study, to have intellectual discourse.
But when the hell are you going to do something?

Caught up now in semantics, a distraction from the work.
Abolition is an act, "I'm going to tear this down!"
But when the hell are you going to do something?
Abolitionists do two things: destroy and then rebuild.

Abolition is an act, "I'm going to tear this down."
Everyone wants to do the book study, to have intellectual discourse.
Abolitionists do two things: destroy and then rebuild.
Is it education for liberation or liberation education?

Can't be just about the protest and then putting the placard in the garage.
It's all about liberating from oppression.
You have to love Black people.
If you can say all lives matter, but struggle to say black lives matter, then I have to wonder.

It's all about liberation from oppression.
So much was stripped from us, our leadership, mind, and history.
If you can say all lives matter, but struggle to say black lives matter, then I have to wonder.
First of all, you must really desire to tear down to lift up.

So much was stripped from us, our leadership, mind, and history.
You have to love Black people.
First of all, you must really desire to tear down to lift up.

Can't be just about the protest and then putting the placard in the garage.

[In this work] Sometimes the journey is the destination-we need sojourners willing to serve

by Shakira (2022)

We got to get there
our brilliance can't be stifled any longer
radical and filled with momentum
intensity is not an indication of danger

our brilliance can't be stifled any longer
budding change agents are ready to practice using their voices to fight for truth; it will get loud.
intensity is not an indication of danger
there's space for the dissonance, the passion, the brokenness, the beauty yet to come.

budding change agents are ready to practice using their voices to fight for truth; it will get loud.
radical and filled with momentum
there's space for the dissonance, the passion, the brokenness, the beauty yet to come.
we got to get there

Concluding Thoughts

So, can anyone become an abolitionist educator? Maybe not. But should they, yes- whether that is as a co-conspirator or a true abolitionist. If we believe that schools should be a place of joy, of great imagination, of discovery, of possibilities (Dunn et al., 2021; hooks, 1994; Love, 2019; Muhammad, 2020), then "everyone must take part in abolitionist work to address and dismantle the oppressive underpinnings present not only in the institution of education, but society as a whole" (Dunn et al., 2021, p. 216). The opportunity to pause and reflect is not consistently taken in this work due to the prevalent urgency to respond to current demands and produce growth on standardized assessments. The mental health and physical safety demands of leading a campus through COVID's impact has heightened the need to pause and reflect. Adults are often the hardest obstacle in developing mutual spaces of safety and growth for our vulnerable children. Children navigating trauma, display their vulnerability by pushing boundaries to see if the adults are truly invested and engaged, or simply for-a-moment participants in their journey of metamorphosis and self-discovery.

Found poetry can serve as a grounding practice, as well as a platform to hear a voice that evokes emotion, connection, and understanding (Bhattacharya, 2013; Wiggins, 2011). Stovall (2018) characterizes abolitionist educators around actions of challenging corporate charters taking over marginalized communities and high-stakes assessments, supporting community-centered learning spaces, as well as establishing spaces to grow and support radical educators. Many of these themes surfaced within the kitchen-table transcripts and participants' found poetry. These themes influenced the following recommendations for current and future abolitionist educators:

- Find opportunities to honor diverse student voices in your building.
- Understand that the balance between institutional systems and capitalism make creating system shifts difficult for most educators.
- Abolitionist work can be uneasy work—there is a valid fear of being fired for disrupting the system.
- Lead from a value lens; Consider how has your leadership through COVID impacted your students' vision and value systems.
- Minimize harm.
- And most importantly, love has a necessary place in our schools; the type of love that understands the urgency of the work, and values every child.

This work can be done. But it cannot be done in isolation.

Educator Haiku

by April J. Mouton

Pause, reflect, invite
You are more than enough, for
Answers in and with

REFERENCES

Barragán Goetz, P. (2020). *Reading, writing, and revolution: Escuelitas and the emergence of a Mexican American identity in Texas.* University of Texas Press.

Bhattacharya, K. (2013). Voices lost and found: Using found poetry in qualitative research. In *Arts-based research in education* (pp. 101–106). Routledge.

Bolding, A. C., Glover, K. T., Mouton, A. J., & Routt, J. D. (2022). Spades, dominoes, and hot combs: the kitchen-table talk that is necessary to redesign our PK–12 schools. *International Journal of Leadership in Education*, 1–17. https://doi.org/10.1080/13603124.2022.2037157

Butler-Kisber, L. (2002). Artful portrayals in qualitative inquiry: The road to found poetry and beyond. *Alberta Journal of Educational Research, 48*(3). https://doi.org/10.11575/ajer.v48i3.54930

Butler-Kisber, L. (2010). *Qualitative inquiry: Thematic, narrative and arts-informed perspectives*. SAGE.

Center for Disease Control and Preventions (CDC). (2020, December 10). *Disparities in deaths: Racial and ethnic health disparities*. https://www.cdc.gov/coronavirus/2019-ncov/ community/ health-equity/racial-ethnic-disparities/disparities-deaths.html

Creswell, J. W. (2016). *30 essential skills for qualitative research*. SAGE.

Dillard, C. B., & Neal, A. (2020). I am because we are: (Re)membering Ubuntu in the pedagogy of Black women teachers from Africa to America and back again. *Theory Into Practice, 59*(4), 370-378.

Dunn, D. C., Chisholm, A., Spaulding, E., & Love, B. L. (2021). A radical doctrine abolitionist education in hard times. *Educational Studies, 57*(3), 211–223.

Eisner, E. W. (1997). The promise and perils of alternative forms of data representation. *Educational researcher, 26*(6), 4–10.

Guajardo, F., & Guajardo, M. (2013). The power of plática. *Reflections, 13*(1).

Haberman, M. (1991). The pedagogy of poverty versus good teaching. *Phi Delta Kappan, 73*(4), 290–294.

Haddix, M., McArthur, S. A., Muhammad, G. E., Price-Dennis, D., & Sealey-Ruiz, Y. (2016). At the kitchen table: Black women English educators speaking our truths. *English Education, 48*(4), 380.

Hammond, Z. (2014). *Culturally responsive teaching and the brain: Promoting authentic engagement and rigor among culturally and linguistically diverse students*. Corwin Press.

Hoffman, J. W., & Martin, J. L. (2020). Abolitionist teaching in an urban district: A literacy coup. *Urban Education*. https://doi.org/10.1177/0042085920943

hooks, b. (1994). *Teaching to transgress*. Routledge.

Israel, Y. (2021). Dave Chappelle is oblivious to his own blind spots. *The Atlantic*. https://www.theatlantic.com/ideas/archive/2021/11/dave-chappelle-the-closer-lgbtq-race/620741/

Kendi, I. X. (2019). *How to be an antiracist*. One World.

Lathan, S. (Director). (2021). *Dave Chappelle: The Closer* [Film]. Netflix.

Love, B. L. (2020). Teachers, we cannot go back to the way things were. *Education Week*. https://www.edweek.org/leadership/opinion-teachers-we-cannot-go-back-to-the-way-things-were/2020/04

Love, B. (2019). *We want to do more than survive: Abolitionist teaching and the pursuit of educational freedom*. Beacon Press.

Mapping Police Violence. (2022, January 20). *Mapping police violence*. https://mappingpoliceviolence.org/

McKinney de Royston, M. (2020). Black womanist teachers' political clarity in theory and practice. *Theory Into Practice, 59*(4), 379–388.

Meier, D., & Gasoi, E. (2017). *These schools belong to you and me: Why we can't afford to abandon our public schools.* Beacon Press.

Moses, R. P., & Cobb, C. E. (2001). *Radical equations: Civil rights from Mississippi to the algebra project.* Beacon Press.

Moore, D. L. (2018) Black radical love: A practice. *Public Integrity, 20*(4), 325–328. https://doi.org/10.1080/10999922.2018.1439564

Morris, M. (2016). *Pushout: The criminalization of Black girls in schools.* The New Press.

Morrison, L. (2020). Principals: Check on your Black staff. We are not ok. *The Educator's Room.* https://theeducatorsroom.com/principals-check-on-your-black-staff-we-are-not-ok/

Muhammad, G. (2020). *Cultivating genius: An equity framework for culturally and historically responsive literacy.* Scholastic.

National Center for Education Statistics (NCES). (2019, February). *Indicator 15: Retention, suspension, and expulsion.* https://nces.ed.gov/programs/raceindicators/indicator_rda.asp

Neal, A. M., & Dunn, D. C. (2020). Our ancestors' wildest dreams: (Re)membering the freedom dreams of Black women abolitionist teachers. *Journal of Curriculum Theorizing, 35*(4).

Oluo, I. (2019). *So you want to talk about race.* Hachette.

Patrick, L. D. (2016). Found poetry: Creating space for imaginative arts-based literacy research writing. *Literacy Research: Theory, Method, and Practice, 65*(1), 384–403.

Payne, C. M. (2008). *So much reform, so little change: The persistence of failure in urban schools.* Harvard Education Press.

Pithouse-Morgan, K. (2016). Finding myself in a new place: Exploring professional learning through found poetry. *Teacher Learning and Professional Development, 1*(1), 1–18.

Riley, K., & Solic, K. (2021). Abolitionist teacher education in the contact zone: Tensions of facilitating teacher candidate learning in activist educator spaces. *Equity & Excellence in Education, 54*(2), 1–13.

Sharpless, R. (2007). The history of oral history. In T. L. Charlton, L. E. Myers, & R. Sharpless (Eds.), *History of oral history: Foundations and methodology* (pp. 9–32). Altamira Press.

Simmons, D. (2019). How to be an antiracist educator. *ASCD Education Update, 61*(10). https://www.ascd.org/el/articles/how-to-be-an-antiracist-educator

Sjollema, S. D., Hordyk, S., Walsh, C. A., Hanley, J., & Ives, N. (2012). Found poetry–Finding home: A qualitative study of homeless immigrant women. *Journal of Poetry Therapy, 25*(4), 205–217.

Stovall, D. (2018). Are we ready for 'school' abolition? Thoughts and practices of radical imaginary in education. *Taboo: The Journal of Culture and Education, 17*(1), 6.

The Equity Collaborative. (n.d.). *A partial timeline of educational oppression in the U.S.: Adapted from the national equity project.* http://theequitycollaborative.com/wp-content/uploads/2017/09/Education-Timeline-Handout.pdf

Virella, P. (2021). Cause you talk like me. In J. A. Alston, L. Scott, & S. N. Alexander (Eds.), *Purveyors of change: School leaders of color share narratives of student, school, and community success* (pp. 37–40). Information Age Publishing.

Wiggins, J. (2011). Feeling it is how I understand it: Found poetry as analysis. *International Journal of Education & the Arts, 12*(LAI 3). https://www.researchgate.net/publication/292984881_Feeling_it_is_how_I_understand_it_Found_Poetry_As_Analysis

CHAPTER 12

CLOSURE

Darin A. Thompson

March of 2020 signaled a historical shift in K–12 education that came with a bevy of challenges. This shift was attributed to the COVID-19 pandemic. The challenges that the pandemic presented impacted not only people personally, but the challenges also exposed the inequities existing in K-12 education. The pandemic similarly presented significant changes to the way schools operate in educating students.

Regarding the personal impact, many encountered life-changing experiences as the pandemic impacted them financially. The quality of life for people was adversely impacted by the pandemic. Families also experienced unexpected deaths due to the pandemic. The traumatic impact of the pandemic left many students and their families with significant needs that required a very targeted focus on comprehensive wraparound supports and services. Students and educators both were presented with challenges that included navigating and responding to the political climate around issues of race during the time. Issues related to access to technology, navigating online platforms, adjusting to new modes of delivery of instruction, ever-evolving operational procedures, contact tracing protocols, and the frustration of adjusting to what people often have referred to as the "new normal" presented even more complexities to the existing equation.

This book has highlighted several responses by aspiring leaders to the personal impact of the pandemic that encompass a focus on compassion, empathy, and self-care. Aspiring leaders also placed a premium on establishing a work-life balance, collaboration, staying connected, and building strong positive relationships throughout their buildings to prevent staff and students from becoming further isolated in response to the pandemic. Furthermore, aspiring leaders found themselves confronting equity issues that surfaced during the pandemic through acknowledging a need for courageous dialogue around issues of race in schools, advancing social justice efforts, and centering instructional leadership upon promoting experiences that validated and affirmed the cultural identities of all students. School leaders were also forced to make significant adjustments to how they lead post-pandemic. Many of these changes were operationally focused, along with having to focus on shifting leadership orientations towards change and crisis management. There was also a need to redefine teacher expectations in this regard.

Like what aspiring leaders in this book have shared, as a practicing principal, I was also faced with similar challenges. In response, I had to ensure that my leadership focused on equivalent aspects such as empathy, strengthening relationships, collaboration, high levels of support, communication, educational equity, and operations. Moreover, I focused on key aspects of transformational leadership and culturally responsive school leadership (CRSL) in my focus. In terms of transformational leadership, my focus was on paradigm-shifting, while providing high levels of support to staff, being collaborative with staff, and embracing innovation. In this regard. In terms of CRSL, I focused on critical self-reflection and promoting a culturally responsive and inclusive school environment. Both leadership frameworks allowed me to uniquely address the personal impact the pandemic had on staff and students, advance educational equity, and adjust to operational changes as a school.

To address the personal impact people were experiencing in my school community, I leveraged our school-based intervention team and our school counseling department to be more centered on comprehensive wraparound support for families and centered on responding to the mental health issues that our students were experiencing. Additionally, I concentrated on keeping my staff motivated during the pandemic. Hence, we built collective efficacy around rededicating ourselves to our school's vision and to our why as a team. Furthermore, my leadership approach placed a premium on affording grace to my staff and students, being flexible with them, being in tune with the human element of the job and finding ways to avoid loading my staff up with things to do. I also placed an emphasis on self-care and replenishment by allowing people to fully disconnect when away from work. This meant that we did not send emails after work hours. We conducted meetings during the instructional day inside of contractual hours. I also established a "Genius Hour" during the day for my administrative team. This was an hour of uninterrupted time each day for my administrative team to be dedicated to personal professional learning or to engage in deep work. I personally used that time to engage in reflection specific to what my staff needed to fully adjust to the impact of the pandemic and to continue to feel empowered and supported. Finally, to further keep everyone motivated, supported, and connected to soften the blow of the personal impact of the pandemic, I created more opportunities for staff to dialogue with one another outside of the standard meetings. As a leadership team, we instituted weekly departmental check-ins, along with optional staff meetings to create more opportunities to provide support, discuss concerns, and develop solutions to enhance instruction and make the job easier to navigate. Coincidingly, we created opportunities for interdepartmental collaboration through a professional learning pathways model. This model focused on having staff from various departments form professional learning networks to work on group research projects that served to enhance instructional delivery. The groups presented their research findings to the staff. The topics included building relationships with students, culturally responsive teaching, and data analysis and intervention.

In terms of addressing equity issues in my school post-pandemic. I leveraged CRSL in multiple ways. More specifically, I concentrated on critical self-reflection as the first pillar of CRSL to gauge whether we were arresting or promoting oppressive practices that contribute to the marginalization of certain student groups. I also focused on promoting culturally responsive and inclusive environments as the second pillar of CRSL. Under that second pillar, our school formed an equity committee to serve as an entity for collecting data on our current state of equity and to develop an action plan/social justice agenda to advance educational equity in our school to develop a warm, welcoming, and inclusive school environment. Our equity team also used empathy audits to guide work around creating a more inclusive environment for our students. Post pandemic, our instructional leadership team led efforts around shifting grading practices away from traditional models that encompass three categories of failure and moving towards more equitable grading practices. As an administrative team, we targeted addressing the subjective nature of certain disciplinary infractions such as defiance and disrespect. Instead of an out-of-school suspension being the default for these types of conduct infractions, we leveraged restorative practices instead to avoid criminalizing culture and instituting exclusionary practices.

In terms of operations, the pandemic shifted the way business was done for many educators and shifted what 21st century leadership looked like. More specifically, there was no educational preparation or leadership coaching that had taken place to prepare school leaders for the shift. In response, our school tried to make operational items and protocols as plug-and-play as possible by providing step-by-step informational loom videos. We held frequent optional staff meetings to highlight logistical and operational items, including navigating new modes of instructional delivery through online platforms, contact tracing and COVID mitigation protocols. I also created a live FAQ document with links to procedures and protocols around those operational and logistical items to serve as a one-stop-shop for quick and easy access to information for staff.

As illustrated throughout this book, the effects of the pandemic have stretched educators to a level of tapping into innovative practices that will forever change the landscape of how we do business in K–12 education. I hope this book offers experiences and insight to support leaders worldwide in continuing to promote excellence in their schools operationally and instructionally, providing the necessary support to staff and school communities, and advancing equitable educational experiences for students and their families despite the challenges posed by the pandemic.

ABOUT THE EDITORS

Patricia M. Virella is an Assistant Professor in the Department of Educational Leadership at Montclair State University. Dr. Virella's research focuses on implementing equity-oriented leadership through leader responses. Dr. Virella also studies equity-oriented crisis leadership examining how school leaders can respond to crises without further harming marginalized communities. Finally, Dr. Virella studies Puerto Rico's education system and the current reform law.

Nathan Tanner is a PhD Candidate in Education Policy, Organization and Leadership at the University of Illinois at Urbana-Champaign. An emerging educational historian and policy scholar, Nathan's research critically examines the politics of place, race(ism), and religion in the construction of educational and schooling configurations for, and the experiences of, Black and Indigenous youth in the American West, past and present.

Darin A. Thompson is a speaker, trainer, coach, and author in the field of K–12 school leadership. Dr. Thompson is also the CEO of Pivotal Leaders Group, LLC. Prior to starting Pivotal Leaders Group, Dr. Thompson served as a middle and high school Principal with diverse experiences in rural, urban, and suburban school districts. In those experiences, Dr. Thompson has led several major school initiatives that enhanced equity and expanded access to opportunity for all students. In his roles, Dr. Thompson's leadership approach has positively influenced school culture, team dynamics, and improved educational outcomes for students.

Printed in the USA
CPSIA information can be obtained
at www.ICGtesting.com
LVHW080019141023
760425LV00002B/80